WHO KILLED LANA B?
The Inside Story of Domestic Violence

WHO KILLED LANA B?
The Inside Story of Domestic Violence

By Millie Bianco

National Victims Advocate

This book is dedicated with love and honor
to my daughter, Lisa,
who never stopped fighting the good fight
while becoming a good mother and working
for her sister victims,

and to those who fight in the trenches for victims
with only one agenda:
to improve the human condition

Contents

Foreword

June 1991 ... Thirteen months after Lana's murder

To My Daughter, Lana:

Lana, your life now is a series of papers, photographs, and newspaper clippings. First, your birth certificate, then pictures of a beautiful little girl with big brown eyes peeking out from under the brim of a pink bonnet. Your report cards, showing already your drive to earn good grades. The pictures of you in your lacy first communion dress and veil, your chubby pre-teen years and the teens. Then your marriage license.

Now the copies of police reports amidst the birth certificates of your two beautiful daughters. So many for you in the small city of Marietta, Indiana. Your application for work-study programs and scholarships, preparations for earning your degrees. Your divorce papers. More police reports. Restraining orders, the copy of *Who's Who in American Colleges* with your name in it.

Your pink name card from your position at the women's shelter. Finally, your death certificate. It describes in graphic detail the atrocities inflicted upon your poor, defenseless body that led to your death.

I am now all about Lana Bordolos—dealing with your/our children and your notoriety. I hardly remember the funeral and don't know when I will have time to properly deal with your loss except for the occasional private momements of screaming and wall-pounding.

I can only do all that I can for your children and you, and for as many women as I can help, for as long as I can. I will try to document, for you and your children, what, if any, benefits your death may have bought to others. I'll do this to try to give your death some meaning for your children. But how can I justify it? I must let you know somehow, Lana, how terribly embarrassed, ashamed, and sorry I am that in spite of your strength, spirit, determination, and pain, the system chose indifference. Know that your spirit lives on.

Love always,

Mom

If a person has had a unique experience, it is his or her obligation to share it with others, so that they may learn what isn't in the textbooks. This book is written to show how the realities differ from the ideologies of domestic violence prevention. It is written to answer those who would ask, "Why doesn't she just leave?"

Lana did leave, even though in domestic abuse cases, FBI statistics show that when she does, the odds of her being murdered increase tremendously, especially in the first few months, over those who stay. It is written to show that even though many people said after Lana's murder there were two people who failed her: the officials at the Department of Corrections who released her ex-husband that fateful day. But, clearly that's not the case. It took a nation to fail her. This is not a case of revenge or anger; I wrote it to show where the inadequacies are in the system and to tell the inside story, a story born of experience, considered opinions, and research.

This will not be entirely about statistics. When it comes to statistics, we must consider their sources, as they might be skewed. Most of the statistics found here come from government Web sites because it seems unlikely that the government has an axe to grind or a reason to shrink or inflate figures to make a point. We all know that thousands of women are beaten and murdered by intimate partners every day. According to FBI Uniform Crime Statistics, about 1,500 women are killed by their husbands or boyfriends each year. The reason we don't realize this is that each woman dies one at a time. Each year, a minimum of two million women are abused. A search of the Web reveals that many of the figures used in various Web sites involving domestic violence studies are very outdated and indicate a lack of attention to the topic. Political correctness and reverence will not be a priority here because this work comes from intense personal experience. It includes my role as my grandchildren's guardian in the aftermath of my daughter's death, as well as the continued existence of an old boy's club. Legislation and active enthusiasts at the federal level are critical, as they are at all levels, but federal bills call for the highest level of accountability. Women have made some strides, but they are far from having achieved equality.

PROLOGUE: The Murder

May 5, 1990

Lee pulled her car up behind the ambulance in front of Lana's home. She got out of the car with shaking legs, told the policeman nearest her, "I'm Lana's mother. I want to see her." The view across the street was blocked, the doors of the ambulance open, but no one was inside. She could not see Lana and was unaware that she was lying across the street, dead.

The policeman stared blankly at her.

"I'm Lana's mother, and I want to see her," she repeated, becoming more alarmed. "Where is she?"

A strange look came over the policeman's face. He seemed unable to respond, and eventually blurted out, "Well ma'am, he shot and bludgeoned her to death."

Lee heard a scream in her ears that seemed to come from the depths of the earth and rise to the heavens. She distinctly remembered that in the midst of that scream, the thought came over her, "Free at last, my darling daughter, free at last."

That's what it can come to for victims of domestic violence and their families: the final release from stalking, beating, harassment, and victimization is death. She felt her knees going out from underneath her and someone supporting her and saying, "The girls need you."

On this May afternoon, Lana had just gotten out of the tub, preparing to go to her aunt and uncle's twenty-fifth wedding anniversary party. Suddenly there was the sound of breaking glass as her ex-husband broke in through the back door. She screamed at her daughter, Brittany, who was then ten years old, to go next door and call the police. Her other daughter, six-year old Alicia, was upstairs playing with her dolls. What happened after that is unknown. What is known is that, as she had instructed so many of her clients at the women's shelter to do, Lana managed to get outside. Her ex-husband ran after her, and at a neighbor's front door, he brutally murdered her.

CHAPTER 1: The Abuse

Lana B.

Lee's goal in life had been the typical 1950s goal of many women: to be married and raise happy, healthy, well-adjusted children, structuring her life around them and her husband. Lee thought she had achieved that goal. A year after her high school graduation, she fell in love and soon married Vincente. He was tall and slender with dark good looks and sculptured features and a head of wavy, thick hair. The physical attraction was strong. He was an engineer who commuted from their hometown to Chicago, where he worked for a prestigious firm. Her daughter, Lana, was born the following year. A son, Mason, was her second child. Another son, Marty, was her youngest. She would lie in bed and remember that in her nightly prayers, the only thing she had asked of God was to not let anything happen to her children.

First it had been Marty who was killed in a single-car accident when he was just sixteen years old, not a block away from home. Marty, who had never had a traffic ticket or accident. He had lain in the intensive care unit of the hospital for ten days. The whole time she pleaded and tried to bargain with God to save his life, but Marty never regained consciousness. One morning when she was alone with him, exercising his legs and arms, he heaved a sigh and just stopped breathing.

Lee and Vincente decided to donate organs. They donated the kidneys, and the most difficult for Lee, his eyes. Marty had such beautiful, soulful, caramel-colored eyes. Later, she received a very meaningful letter telling the family that Marty's kidneys had been successfully transplanted into two patients. But, oh, the eyes; never any word about the eyes or how someone might be viewing the world with Marty's dying gift. Lee would never forgive that, or perhaps herself, for the donation.

The grief of a mother is a complicated agony. There is guilt, incomprehension, loss, denial, shock, and agony. It was an agony so torturous that she prayed for some horrible physical pain to change the focus of her suffering. Having lived through it five years before, she now realized that it was just a prelude to the way Lana met her death. Considering the aftermath of her prayers, she decided that she wouldn't depend on God for divine intervention..

Lana entered the world as Lee's firstborn, weighing a scant five pounds. Always of tiny stature, she reached a full 5'2" at maturity. She had the coloring, eyes, and dark hair of her Mediterranean heritage on her father's side. She had large brown eyes with long lashes, a beautiful smile, and a soft, loving nature. She grew up in an average, middle class two-parent family. Lana was intellectually quick and could manage good grades without much effort. She had planned to attend college and eventually get her own apartment and have a career. She was always very independent.

Lana's plans for college went out the window when she began, at the age of seventeen, to be wooed by a tall, blond, charming man ten years her senior. His name was Adam Portland. He was a local in the suburban community where they lived.

As Lana's parents, Lee and Vince did not approve of the relationship between their daughter and Adam because of the age difference, although Lana had always seemed mature and related well to those who were older. For the next year, her parents did the dance of trying to make her aware of potential problems, while being careful of pressing the issue to the point where she would become more involved with him in his defense. This became more of an issue when they found out that he was divorced from his first wife, and accelerated when they found out that he had been in jail for car theft. But in the end, his power to manipulate and influence Lana won out. After all, he treated her like a queen and showered her with expensive gifts, and he loved his dog. They were married almost immediately after Lana's graduation from high school. The year was 1978. Lana was just eighteen.

It is often the case that a seemingly loving and caring person is also a wonderful con, masquerading evil as love. During one violent assault on her, Lana asked him why he was doing this to her. His reply was that it was because he loved her. Was this violent act he called love an out-of-control confusion of his insecurity and need to possess, control, and dominate by any means available?

Adam Portland fooled many people, mostly men. At the outset, men are fused in the "brotherhood system." How else does one explain the following report submitted by a Marietta policeman?

The report, written after Adam broke into her house, stated that Adam had kicked in the door, slapped her in the face, then went outside and blocked her car from leaving. In the report, the officer writes: *"complainant got too close and got slapped."*

It's called victim-blaming. This report was only one among many that Lana made against him for death threats, firebombing her garage, rape, assault, and kidnapping of the children—all this while restraining orders were on file. Adam had laughed when they were filed and considered them nothing but pieces of paper. Proving a violation was just another matter of his word against hers. There were many instances in which police reports were not filed because they were called civil complaints. Meanwhile, Adam constantly conjured up charges of child abuse against Lana and reported them to any and every child abuse and child neglect agency. He conspired with a business partner in drawing up forged legal documents against her. There was one Marietta policeman who claimed after Lana's death that he had responded many times to calls at her house and stated that he would like to be the one to pull the switch when/if Adam Portland were executed. But there were no reports in the file with his name on them.

It is imperative that police be educated in the areas of domestic violence. They are, not surprisingly, reluctant to enter a situation, especially when the chances of getting hurt are high. Or they may be biased. This why it is so important to have a domestic violence intervention program in place—something akin to the Duluth model which employs the directive to intercede from the time of the first incident, with a comprehensive follow-through program that makes the abuser accountable for his actions from that first incident, and then monitors the steps he and she take following the incident. There is no consistency, statewide or nationally, for dealing with this problem.

On Gender Perspective

On first becoming embroiled in Lana's struggles, Lee had been naïve in thinking that there was justice in the law and that there was equality between the sexes. She soon came to realize that she had been wrong.

Laws on the books stated that women had once been chattel, along with their husband's cattle and hogs. Laws on the books had declared the length of the stick with which a woman could be beaten. Vestiges of those attitudes are still alive and well today. Nationally, it took over a hundred years for women to attain the right to vote.

While some of these old laws may no longer appear on the books, the attitude of male superiority lives on, as though inherently encased in a recessive gene. It is reflected in the glass ceiling of the workplace, in the disparity of pay for equal work, and in the halls of justice. These are the persons entrusted with the protection of what is termed the weaker sex. This is not to say that there are not many kind and gentle men, but it is not likely in this enlightened age that one can dispute the fact that the male, in general, has more aggressive, proprietary, and territorial tendencies. If Lana were to attempt a divorce, Adam would beat her, hide the children from her, and slander her reputation. He told Lana that if she left him, she would be buried beside her brother who had been killed in an automobile accident five years earlier. Ultimately, he kept that promise. However, Lee and Vincente knew little about Adam's behavior until the police became involved, or Lana was hospitalized. Like many women, Lana did not want her parents to know how wrong her choice was. Unlike some women, Lana had strong family support, an alternate housing situation, and an attorney. Neither had she witnessed domestic violence in the home she grew up in. She used every avenue she could to help herself, but to little avail. Law dispensed from the law library cannot relate to a woman being hunted by a man with an obsession. How much influence Adam's parents exerted over him wasn't clear—the families only saw each other at the wedding. One thing is certain, Adam's mother counted on him for support, maintenance of their home, and believed everything he told her and followed any directive he gave her. She was often involved in his misdeeds. She was a participant in his abduction of Brittany and Alicia and left the telling message on Lana's telephone anwering machine "I hope you get what you deserve, you bitch."

Something else the law doesn't take into consideration: men's built-in, sometimes almost mindless, sex drive. While nature built this drive into both men and women in order to perpetuate the continuation of the species, some men are driven more by these urges. History supports this aggressive tendency. When we look at media coverage of rape, abductions, serial killers, mass murderers, child molestations, pornography, and so on, we see the way these aggressive tendencies can dominate men. One needs only to follow the media to support this opinion. This should not to be construed as feminist slandering, merely an acknowledgment of the situation.

For hundreds of years, a man's home has been his castle, even if he is beating the queen. History also shows us that the majority of domestic violence cases were, for the most part, hidden. It was considered a male right and family shame. Even today, there are women who for one reason or another—shame, fear of their abuser, religious convictions, and financial dependence—choose to remain silent. Domestic violence knows no socioeconomic or territorial boundaries. One abuser may use acid to disfigure a woman's face and another will use his fists or a tool. Both actions are to damage her to the point where all other men will refuse her. Why this need to control and dominate; why the regard of a woman as his possession? Why the insecurity? Control, domination, and a need to win may be inherent qualities in some men, tied to their aggression. When coupled with an insecurity complex and/or mental illness, the abuser can dedicate his life to the suffering and hunting his prey, as in Lana's case. This hunt is facilitated by our legal system. It would appear that the majority of perpetrators and their defenders have managed to make domestic violence a "woman's issue," leaving the victims to fight for themselves. This was both Lana's and Lee's opinion, and they guessed, the opinion of many others frustrated with the lack of attention and positive strides in the area of domestic violence.

The Kidnappings and Lee as Mediator

During the times when Adam Portland kidnapped his and Lana's daughters, Lee somehow became mediator between Lana and Adam. Adam had washed dishes in Lee's kitchen when she had family Sunday dinners. He liked her cooking. He saw that she dearly loved the girls and provided a warm, loving, grandmotherly influence. On one occasion when Lee cared for the girls while Adam and Lana went away for a few days, he bought her an expensive leather coat. This was before Lee knew what he was doing to her daughter.

About three years after their marriage, Lana decided to utilize the scholarships she had received at high school graduation and apply for Pell grants to the local university, in addition to some work-study. This, of course, was a threat to Adam's control of her, and, Lee suspected, raised the concern that she would come into contact with people superior to him. Lee had always thought Adam had the most egotistical inferiority complex. It would appear that her enrollment in university precipitated a greater need for control and more use of kidnapping of the children as a bargaining tool.

Whenever Adam abducted the children from Lana, Lee had to balance her desire to get the girls back with the importance of staying as neutral as possible on the phone with him, in order to keep him on the line and record the calls. On one occasion, Adam directed Lee to a phone booth about four miles from the house. The phone booth was located at the corner of two rural highways where one could see the booth and the surrounding area without much problem. She went there, but the phone didn't ring.

After the girls had been gone for two weeks, Adam called to ask Lee if she wanted to see the girls. Of course. Lee was to meet him at the playground of a nearby elementary school—again, a very visible spot. She arrived at the specified time and she listened to Adam complain about the situation. Lee asked nothing more than he was willing to give, and she tried to present herself as the diplomat.

At this meeting, Adam asked Lee to accompany him and the girls to lunch. As she got into his car, she saw a handgun on the floor of the car where she couldn't possibly miss it. They went to a local Marietta restaurant and ordered their food. At the end of the meal, the girls wanted to use the restroom, and as she escorted them, Lee eyed the distance from the restroom to the front door and assessed whether she could escape with them. As soon as she opened the restroom door to leave, she found Adam standing directly in front of it. She didn't know if he had the gun on him or not. They left, and she returned home and he returned to his hiding place with the girls.

During another kidnapping, Adam took the girls to Canada with him, all the while keeping their whereabouts a secret. During his last, and longest, abduction, he took the girls all over the country. He called and told Lee that he was in Mexico. He complained about the fact that no one understood him and about the price of cigarettes. Lee knew that it was physically impossible for him to be in Mexico since he had disappeared just the afternoon before. He hadn't returned the girls following his scheduled visit with them. He had been ordered to pick them up from Lee's home in order to limit contact with Lana. The week prior, he had asked Lee if she would go shopping for clothing for the girls. She gladly agreed and he paid her for them. Little did Lee know that she was outfitting her granddaughters to be abducted.

The following weeks Adam called many times, threatening to take the girls out of the country. During one call, Lee heard what seemed to be the sounds of an airport terminal. There was one big problem with this story: Lee knew Adam was deathly afraid of flying.

During another call, he complained that he was going out of his mind. The girls were jumping up and down on the beds and hanging off the curtains. He described the room as strewn with potato chips and litter.

Lee was never really afraid that he would physically hurt the girls. They could usually wind him around their little fingers. Lee had never seen him physically punish them, and he seemed unable to do that. He had always demonstrated a soft side with the girls, and they seemed to have nothing to do with his issue with Lana. Holding on to this thought securely was the only way Lee and Lana could deal with the situation. But they could not forgive the emotional abuse he inflicted by using the girls as pawns. A local officer, Ken Whittle, helped to bring the girls home. Adam had actually called Whittle, and Whittle kept Adam on the line until the call was traced. Federal agents found him at a condo on the beach in South Carolina. He was arrested and charged with illegal detention.

Adam had to know the call would be traced. It was during this kidnapping, prior to his arrest, that Adam called Lana. Since he had taken the girls out of state, authorities were able to involve the FBI. Someone had tipped Adam off about this, and he was furious. He told Lee during one phone call that if charges kept piling up on him, he would get less time if he just came home and killed Lana. As incredible as that seemed, Lee later learned that the average time of incarceration for domestic murders is eight years, at which time the murderers are often released. Depending on variables such as jurisdiction, judge, jury, etc., it is possible that a longer sentence would be given for a kidnapping.

On the Legal System

Everything Lee had read about people was that they're motivated by two basic drives: the avoidance of pain and the attainment of pleasure. Adam Portland once made this statement to her: "Lee, I've been in the legal system, on the wrong side, for a long time, and I know what I can get away with. The system is behind me." This was his pleasure. Every time he got away with assaulting Lana, every time an officer believed his lies, every time he played the brotherhood game, every time he was able to get a hearing postponed, he felt that the law justified and reinforced his choices. Every time an abuser is not made to suffer the consequences of his actions, he is reinforced. And this was Adam's avoidance of pain.

Lee and Lana and the children were hiding out in a fishing cottage in La Porte, Indiana. They had just come off a week on the road, fleeing Adam's violence. Lana's attorney had advised her to get out of town. They had left like fugitives in the night, under cover of darkness. They stayed in off-the-road motels and at a friend's lake cottage. It was Mother's Day, and while Lee was asleep, Lana managed to get the girls and herself out of the motel room without waking her. When she returned, she had gotten breakfast sandwiches and coffee for all and had presented Lee with a flowered mug as a Mother's Day gift. Lee would treasure it always.

Lana wanted a place to stay that was near enough to Marietta so that she could continue her education at the local university. She went back to the Marietta area wearing wigs and driving friends' cars to avoid being recognized. After one particular beating, Lana was escorted to and from her car by security at her college campus. Lee thought to herself, "My God, I can't believe this is happening in America. If the public knew what their legal system is like, they would be as ashamed and embarrassed as I am." Many years later, Lee still would have difficulty when standing at sporting events and singing about "the land of the free and home of the brave." Lana was not free and her bravery bought her a cemetery plot.

The average American who has not had experience with the system as a victim thinks, "Well, there are laws. He can't do that and get away with it."

But that is not true. He can, and he did.

With each incident, the victim thinks, "*Now* the legal system will take the criminal to task."

Not necessarily. One of the biggest fights against domestic violence is the battle against attitudes. Often the abuser has no other criminal history and appears to be a "good guy," so even if he is prosecuted, he may just get a slap on the wrist. There is a residual tolerance that must not be tolerated. If the judges, prosecutors, prison staff, and police would act as if the woman in danger were their own sister, things might be different. We cannot mandate a caring attitude. That was blatantly evident in Lana's case.

Sometime after Lana's murder, Lee spoke on behalf of a preventive detention of violent offenders bill at the Capitol Building in Indianapolis. This was during her legislative work. Lee's testimony followed that of the Morris County prosecutor. Following his testimony, one of the senators—who was also a judge, and who had once been charged for urinating in the street and public drunkenness— stated that he hoped this bill wouldn't apply to domestic violence because he believed that there are two sides to every story. After Lee's testimony, he left and abstained from voting.

The Senate resolution passed with flying colors, but the next step was the Ways and Means Committee. Lee and the senator she was working with, Joe Zakas, sat in the hearing room long past the appointed time for Lee's testimony to begin. Finally, when she rose to speak, one of the members sitting at the head table left the room. He was a criminal defense lawyer. Another member of the committee stood up, solely to acknowledge Lee's dedication and bravery. Without naming anyone, Lee repeated the senator's response to the bill and agreed that there are two sides to every story. She then asked that if 95–98 percent of the battered and murdered are women, can we really equate those two sides? Another member of the committee, not surprisingly, a woman, remarked on Lee's bravery. The resolution failed.

The laws on the books in Indiana dictated that the only offenses worthy of keeping a person in jail were murder and treason. Furthermore, the governor informed her in a personal letter that there had been an unwritten agreement among legislators negating the passage of any more laws detaining people in prison because of the overcrowding of jails. Thus Adam Portland had been free to hunt at will, as often as he liked.

For hundreds of years we have had groups of well-dressed, well-educated, well-spoken people (almost exclusively men) creating and defeating laws. If the bottom line in criminal defense is money, then how has that affected our legal system and our society in general? When it comes to prosecution, the alleged offender is always told that if he or she cannot afford an attorney, one will be appointed for them. You don't hear that for the victim. The victims are often financially unable to hire an attorney at critical moments. Then Senator and now Vice President Joe Biden recognized this handicap and discussed plans to enlist, train, and place 100,000 domestic violence lawyers as volunteers to ensure that domestic violence victims get the immediate legal assistance they so desperately need. That proposal, Bill S.1515, is no longer current. One of the complaints against it was that it would be just another social dispensation of taxpayer funds. However, if those who held that view considered the legal fees distributed to countless attorneys working continuously for the felons and murderers, even after conviction and incarceration, they might look at it as a source of prevention worth a pound of cure.

Fairness, the principle on which equity is based, has been factored out of the legal system—there is no more right or wrong. Additionally, the wrongdoer is now portrayed as the victim. Theories that attempt to place the blame for character deviations on others have accelerated the abuse of this doctrine. The harm done by good people who embrace bad causes cannot be calculated. This is not to say that others never influence criminal actions, but we cannot remove personal accountability. And personal accountability should extend to the person using that defense. The abuser had all the rights, privileges, benefits and protections built into the system on the criminal's behalf.

Adam Portland was consistently given the opportunity to confront and inflict pain on Lana, but there were no corresponding laws that insured her freedom from those confrontations. Adam did some of his worst damage to Lana while out on bond. During one incident, he tied her wrists and ankles with extension cords, raped and beat her and attempted to choke her with a tie. Immediately after that incident, he took her to his attorney's office where the attorney, seeing Lana's condition, wrote up an agreement for her to sign, stating that she would agree not to prosecute. She never signed. Instead, Lana went to the hospital, and then reported the incident to the prosecutor's office.

Lana had Lee take pictures of the rope burns on her wrists and ankles and her face. The two of them were in the elevator in the County-City Building in Marietta on their way to the prosecuting attorney's office. Lana looked at her mother and smiled that soft, soulful smile of hers through the facial swelling and bruises, and stated quietly but confidently, "This time, Mom, this time."

A prime example of Adam's ability to con and charm was his relationship with a woman who happened to be a cousin of a local county commissioner. She had connections that enabled her to know Lana's every move in the legal process. Because of this, Adam Portland was almost immediately aware of Lana's decision to prosecute, and soon after, Adam nearly ran Lana off the road in attempt to intimidate her into dropping the charges. But she didn't drop them.

Even after Adam Portland's conviction and jail sentence for illegal detention of the children, another local attorney, Rodney Markham, wrote to the courts on Adam's behalf. To describe the incident where Adam bound, raped and beat her, the attorney wrote: "They were probably having a marvelous sex party which got out of hand and now she was trying to lash her ex-husband to death, using the legal system. I have never known Mr. Portland to be anything other than a perfect gentleman. How repulsive."

There was also a letter from Adam's primary attorney stating that he had known both Lana and Adam for a long time, and that her crimes were just as bad as his, but that they had not been detected by the legal system.

What crimes?

There were none. This is just another example of victim-blaming without evidence. How is it that the average citizen cannot slander without potential legal consequences, but it is accepted practice from those sworn to uphold the law? This is what women might expect from those sworn to uphold the law and promote justice. There is no justice, only a criminal's defense and the manipulation of the law, and an "anything goes" attitude.

July 17, 1985, five years prior to Lana's death, Lee wrote and sent this letter.

To: St. James County Court

Approximately six years ago, our daughter's husband made the following remark to us: "You may not be able to get blood out of a turnip, but you sure can make that turnip suffer." Little did we know then that we were to become his turnips.

In January of 1979, Lana, then in the latter part of her first pregnancy, arrived at our home during a blizzard. She had driven her car, which had every window smashed out. She stated that Adam had done it when she informed him that she was filing for divorce. She also stated that he had told her that if she left him, he would see to it that she would not be able to go to work or school and would make her life so miserable that she would wish she were dead.

During one of his recent death threats, he told Lana that she would be buried alongside her brother, the son we lost four years ago. She had, up to this point in time, been attending a local university, and last year she earned a 4.0 grade point average.

We noticed, during visits to her home, kicked-in doors and broken windows. We did not become involved, nor were we aware of any further problems until we learned of the attempt on Lana's life.

Last year, 1984, on the day that she was to institute divorce proceedings with Attorney Phillips, Adam brought the children to our home and left. Approximately four hours later, Adam returned to our home to pick up the girls. I asked him where Lana was, and he mumbled something and hurried out. That evening, we learned of the assault. The following day his mother called me and wanted to know what had happened at her house. She stated that Lana and Adam had come in, Adam had ordered her to leave, and that when she returned, she found a window broken and "blood all over the place."

The next incident was when Adam, who had taken the girls under the pretense that he was taking them out for ice cream, phoned and told Lana that she would never see them again. We drove over to the house Adam was staying in. We saw the girls in the window, arms outstretched and crying, and Adam's mother pulling them back. The Marietta police who were called to the scene said that since custody hadn't been yet determined, he had every right to them. They were taken without clothing, toys, or anything familiar. They were gone for weeks.

Lana stated that Adam told her later that they had been with the girlfriend of a "cop that he had something on."

At the next hearing, because of the allegations, temporary custodial care was given to me. As Adam walked past me, he laughed. He was given the right to pick them up and return them at appointed times. For the first several visits, everything seemed to go well. Then he asked me if I would shop for clothes for the girls. I very willingly did so, and furnished him with receipts. After the following scheduled pick up, I called in two neighbors to attest to the fact that he did not return the girls. I have since asked them to testify, but they are afraid to give me so much as a notarized statement.

The following morning Adam called me stating that he was in Mexico, with elaborate stories of how expensive the cigarettes were and that no one understood his language. He stated that he had booked a flight to Europe. I knew that it was a physical impossibility for him to be there, since he said that he had driven. I knew he was deathly afraid of flying, but I went along with the story. Negotiations via phone were carried out over the weekend—his directives often changing. Finally, he agreed to bring the children back if we would drop all charges and if Lana would put off the divorce. He got what he wanted. He later told Lana that he had been in Windsor, Ontario. He returned the children in good physical health, aside from marks that appeared to be flea bites.

However, the then five-year-old told me, "Daddy says that you and Mommy don't like us anymore." To this day she panics when we are not in the same room where she last saw us. The two-year-old still has a strong dependence on her older sister. The now six-year-old asks us, "Why does Daddy hit Mommy, and why does Daddy take our things?"

In April of this year, I called Lana at work at the *South Bend Tribune*. She stated that Adam had called her to tell her that he and his sister Mary had "cleaned house for her." We found that a basement window had been broken and household goods and furniture of any value, along with her personal items, including clothing, had been trashed. This necessitated her borrowing a winter coat and trying to salvage what she could. I asked her why she didn't call the police. She said that the usual program would be for them to tell her that it was her word against his, and then he would then do something worse.

The last assault took place shortly after that and was witnessed by our daughter-in-law and two others.

There was no way to deal with him since he was unhampered by morals, ethics, reality, or truth. Additionally, our hands were tied by a system that allows no expedient relief. Lana, the children, and I left town under cover of darkness like fugitives—staying in motels until we could find a place where we thought he might not find her before the final divorce hearing.

During the past two months, we have been inundated with bizarre letters full of threats, demands, and ridiculous accusations. One of these letters was dated only two and a half weeks after the attempt on her life. Adam states in the letter that Lana, (5'2") broke into his home on Merridale Street and performed oral sex on him (6'3") against his will. Copies of these letters allegedly sent to the court seem to be just another attempt to antagonize the family. None of his charges seems to have ever seen the light of day. In another letter to us, he attempts to bargain away all rights to his children if all his demands are met, including the paying of his attorney's fees, which are currently $3,000. Signed copies of all his correspondence are in our possession.

I am in no way being dramatic when I pray for assistance in stopping this lunacy in the name of revenge. Our personal lives and health and business have been greatly affected by all this, and we want nothing but to be left alone and allowed to help reintroduce our daughter and grandchildren to a normal and respectable life.

Several years ago, we loaned Adam $1,200 to get out of jail on an unrelated charge. What a tragic mistake. Adam came to our home several months ago wanting us to "get up" $5,000 so that he could get out of town because he said he wasn't going to jail again for anyone. Lana asked him about his children. He stated that we (Lana's parents) would take care of them. This is the father who is currently fighting for custody.

> Respectfully submitted,
> Lee Bordolos (Signed)
> Vincente Bordolos (Signed)

Court-Appointed Psychologists

The appointed psychologist, Charles Barens, PhD, wrote a letter to Adam Portland's attorney, prior to his sentencing, which sent him to jail. His letter stated that Adam was initially interviewed "while incarcerated in the St. James County Jail" and was given a psychological test that revealed that his behavior was not adequately goal-directed. Social withdrawal, cognitive confusion, anxiety, and depression were the most prominent characteristics Barens observed. It was quite clear that he was not able to trust anyone, and he showed significant degrees of anger and hostility. Initial DSM III diagnosis was 295.40, Schizophreniform disorder.

The next paragraph, while matching the previous paragraphs in size and font, appears on the photocopy of this document to differ in background as well as in sharpness and clarity of print, as though it had been added or transposed. The letter continued, "Mr. Portland was seen in my office on September 26, 1985, at which time it became more obvious that in order for him to optimally benefit from therapy, both he and his former wife should be in treatment."

Any meeting at which Adam could find Lana was an opportunity to run down or harass her. She did go to one meeting, but the state wasn't paying for her, nor had she been ordered. She wasn't the one who needed to be there.

In another paragraph, Barens states, "Since she was not in therapy, it did not seem advisable to continue seeing Mr. Portland." More victim-blaming. Even though in a later proceeding he testified that Adam and Lana came in and he saw that she had been beaten.

Lee met some of the psychologists who were called upon and appointed to the courts. She would meet them at different political functions. While discussing her situation with them, they would make remarks like, "Hey, I don't get paid," and, "I have a family and life to protect." They seemed to empathize with Barens.

Suspected criminals who are considered to be dangerous are shuffled through the system, and if doctors fear retaliation on themselves or their families, they will either provide the most neutral evidence or shift the blame to the victim.

In his final paragraph, Dr. Barens wrote, "Mr. Portland was seen again to discuss the content of this report. He appeared in good spirits and was adequately goal-directed. He mentioned that some unresolved problems with his former wife existed, but at this time these could not be fully worked out due to her reluctance to discuss those differences. Overall, it appeared that things were going as well as expected."

The differences were, of course, the beatings, rapes, kidnapping of the children, firebombing of her garage, and death threats. Adam Portland's behavior, not hers. What was there to discuss? The bias of the police, the pleabargaining, Adam's lawyers continually freeing him from the consequences of his actions? It was evident that he was not going to stop. Women are told to leave and get away; now Dr. Barens was blaming Lana for doing just that. Dr. Barens refused to testify at the trial that later sent Adam Portland to prison, telling Lana that he was afraid. Following Lana's murder, he moved far away from the area.

On Pleabargaining: Part I

I don't think there could be a more eloquent argument against pleabargaining than the following excerpt from Lana's letter to the courts dated May 1988. Pleabargaining is dangerous in situations of domestic violence, especially when prior proof of violence is inadmissible at trial. Lana wrote:

"This letter is in regard to my victim impact statement as requested by the Probation Department for case No.C46578-223-47, State of Indiana vs. Adam Portland.

First, let me state that the plea agreement arranged in relation to these charges was not entirely to my satisfaction. I believed that the second charge of burglary should not have been dropped since it occurred at a different date, place, and time. The charge filed by the State was "Burglary with the Intent to commit Intimidation." In my opinion, I believe that it should have been charged as attempted murder. My reason is that Adam broke into my home, carried a gun, came after me with a rope, kept his suede gloves on the entire time he was in my home and intimidated me to the point that I lost all control of my bodily functions. He also attempted to rape me again. Had his pants not tangled around his ankles causing him to fall, I would never have made it upstairs to my children; because I was able to do so, I am still alive today.

Adam had the motive for murder—he did not want to be convicted of rape. He must have been watching the house, since the night he attacked me was the night I had returned home after being out of town for a few days. I am quite certain Adam had planned to kill me due to the way he talked, his refusal to let me turn any lights on, his constant pacing and looking out the front window, not removing his gloves when I requested him to do so, as well as bringing both a gun and a rope into my home.

This is the second time a charge against him has been dropped. The first time when he raped and beat me. He nearly killed me by wrapping a necktie around my neck as I was choking on my own blood. He proceeded to strangle me until I blacked out and fell. The incident in February of this year also led me to believe he was planning on killing me then since he hid my car, bound my hands and ankles with neckties and an extension cord, in addition to delivering numerous blows to the back of my skull. Had I known the charge would be dropped anyway, I would not have had to endure the horrendous episode I did.

Adam has already told me that if he has to spend any time in jail, he would remember who put him there and he would kill me when he got out. Adam has always been one who must blame others for the predicaments he gets himself into rather than see them as a result of his own actions. In addition, I have a tape in which Adam tells me that the time he would spend in jail for killing me would be minute and well worth it.

I do not perceive these as idle threats.

If you will take the time to look at the enclosed police reports you will see that Adam has quite a history of threatening and violent actions. These seem mild, however compared to current events. As you can see, the tactics he used have accelerated each time. If you are aware of the research done on battery, you will know that it is well-documented that each incident of physical abuse becomes more violent, with the final occurrence resulting in death.

For my own safety, it is inevitable that I must relocate my family before Adam is released from jail. I hope that you will relay to the proper persons just how important it is that I be kept aware of where he is at all times, as well as being given notice of his release date, since I have no choice but to leave behind everything familiar to me in the hope of finding a safe place.

With regard to his sentencing for this particular series of crimes, I was told that his sentence would be between two to eight years. Due to the way in which the prison system is set up, I am also aware that he will serve only half of the time ordered at his sentencing. It is not my nature to wish jail time on anyone; however, due to the constant harassment, threats, fabricated legal charges, physical and emotional damage Adam has caused my family and myself, I pray that he is at least sentenced to the maximum term. The more time he is incarcerated, the more time I will have to finish school, sell my home, find another job, and relocate to a safe place. This may sound selfish; however, considering all the damage he has caused, what my family has been through, and the familial and emotional ties my children and I will have to give up to relocate, I don't think it's too much."

On the day of Lana's murder, Adam Portland turned himself in to a Marietta policeman. His first statement was, "I assume my ex-wife is dead?" He said this with an air of satisfaction, as if a job had at long last been completed.

On Pleabargaining: Part II

After Adam was incarcerated, both Lana and the County Prosecutor requested that the Department of Corrections notify her if Adam was to be released for any reason. He had been assigned to a prison work-release program. As such, prisoners received special privileges and outings. In one such attempt and pass approval, Adam's mother, Janice, had left a phone message for Lana stating that Adam would be getting a pass and that she should get out of town as Adam had blood in his eyes. Lana was able to get that pass blocked. When Adam found out that his mother had made that call, he intimidated her and she left another message for Lana: "I hope you get what you deserve, you bitch."

Adam kept applying and finally succeeded in receiving a pass. There was plenty of evidence of his intention to harm Lana, but with the most violent charges pleabargained away, the prison officials did not think him the threat to her he really was. He left the jail that day in May with his mother and brother, people not even authorized to take him out, supposedly restricted to the Indianapolis area. They then got into the car and drove to the Marietta area, which was five hours away. Adam left his mother at her house. The rest is history. Sometime later, Lee received an anonymous call informing her that the two persons responsible for Adam's release that day had been "kicked upstairs." And so, she was given the impression that the controversial parties were removed from the "hot seat" with a promotion to a higher position within the penal system.

Chapter 2: The Aftermath

Life Must Go On

During the hours following Lana's murder, and while the police were completing their investigation of the crime scene, Brittany, who was just ten years old, pleaded with Lee:, "Why don't they take her to the hospital and try to fix her head?" and, "Why can't they just kill him like he killed her? It's not fair."

Alicia, who was upstairs when Adam broke in, may or may not have seen the murder across the street, but she certainly heard the glass breaking and knew it must have been Daddy—that was his usual mode of entry. She continued playing quietly with a little friend after the murder, evidently blocking everything out. That night the girls went home with Lee to stay.

One morning within two weeks of Adam's incarceration for the murder, the phone rang in Lee's kitchen. She answered and her brain began to reel when she heard Adam's voice. Her mind did not want to conceive what her ears were hearing. He asked to speak to the girls. She told him they weren't home. He then stated that if she didn't stop causing trouble, she was going to be sorry. She told him to talk to a lawyer.

That afternoon a reporter from the *Marietta Tribune* called, and she related the story to her. The story hit the news about a murderer who was able to call from jail and threaten the victim's mother. Then the prosecutor became involved and there was a hearing, and Adam was prohibited from contacting the girls. But Adam continued to harass Lee. He would call someone and tell them to dial Lee's number and then hang up.

Following this, she began to receive mail from him. He stated that she was only the temporary guardian and that wouldn't last long. In another letter, he directs Lee to use his attorney, Carlos Bratton, in a suit against the state for Lana's wrongful death. Lee called the prosecutor's office and was informed that the directive issued only prohibited him from calling the girls, and they could not deny him the right to send mail.

Lee did not want to introduce any more changes into the girls' lives. She received permission to keep them in their current school even though they now lived out of the district, and Lee would need to drive them to school and pick them up each day. She enrolled them in Sunday school and began to make plans for summer camp. She kept them busy doing things kids do. People would always ask her before a play date or party how they should act or treat them, what to say or not say. Lee's reply was to treat them as they would treat any other child. That was the kindest and best directive.

Lee's days were filled with incorporating the children's lives with hers, with constant media requests, and with dealing with the public outrage. She had worked as an office manager for a local temporary service. When her supervisor asked her what she could do to help, Lee asked to be released from her position. All of this was too much to allow her to do anything else and the girls needed her full time. It was so important for her to be there for them. The girls clung to her and it seemed like years before she could use the bathroom without hearing a knock at the door with an accompanying, "Grandma, Grandma?"

All their lives, Lee had loved taking them shopping and decorating cakes for their birthdays and reading to them and taking them out for fun adventures. She had been the fun Grandma. Now that she was the guardian, she wasn't as much fun. She now had to be disciplinarian and enforcer, instill positive work ethics and set an example of how one deals with the worst possible situation with grace. She wanted to see that their physical, emotional, spiritual, and financial lives would be provided for.

For how many years would Adam's actions affect all their lives? It's incalculable—a domino effect, with the last fall always still to come.

Journey for Justice

As the news of Lana's brutal murder swept across the local and national media, an outpouring of sympathy and outrage followed. Some six weeks after the murder, a local radio DJ began a petition drive to go to the state capital. It began as the Purple Ribbon Campaign. Someone had determined that purple was Lana's favorite color, and soon purple ribbons fluttered all over the community and on a good length of the route to Indianapolis.

At the same time, people initiated a petition for stronger laws to protect victims of domestic violence. When this was completed, there were many thousands of signatures over the original goal. Armed with these petitions, Lana's family, representatives of the women's shelter where Lana had worked as a counselor and program director, the DJ (with his remote equipment), and other dignitaries traveled to Indianapolis. They left in a large bus decorated with a large banner that read "Journey for Justice" on the side. A respectable sized caravan followed. On arriving at the capital, the family was ushered into the governor's office for a preparatory meeting before going to the gallery for the presentation of the signed petitions.

Lee distinctly remembered meeting the governor's eyes—long enough for her to transmit the unspoken message, "Yes, we will use each other." Adam's release from prison on a pass and Lana's murder *had* happened on *the governor's* watch. They went out to the gallery ceremony where Governor Billingsley received the petitions and presented Lee with a scroll proclaiming April 24, the day of Lana's birthday, as the official "Lana Bordolos Day" in the state of Indiana. She would have been thirty years of age.

The Media

Lee was often asked to do local television interviews. Sometimes the requests for a filmed interview gave her only half an hour before the film crew arrived. Sometimes she wondered if they thought she sat around the house coiffed, dressed, and in full makeup at all times. At any and all of these interviews, the girls were away, in their rooms, or in the downstairs family room. Lee never allowed the media to photograph or interview them. This was well known among the media and the word got around and was respected. There was no sitting on her doorstep for interviews, always a courteous advance call. She had established herself as a cooperative interviewee.

The first television interview she granted shortly after Lana's murder showed a well-dressed, composed woman who stated that Lana's children were the product of an intelligent and loving mother and gave assurance that they would overcome this. Lee was able to disassociate herself from the rage and anguish that she felt. Perhaps this was counter to the stereotypical images people have of victims of domestic violence. Many people are unaware that domestic violence knows no social, economic, or cultural boundaries. They think that it is more the milieu of the lower classes. Lana had been an attractive, self-educated woman who had used her degrees to help other victims of domestic violence and she had two beautiful little girls. Over the years, all events associated with the murder were closely monitored by the community and surrounding area. Lee had a sympathetic audience and she was able to speak with insight, and without anger. In the January, 1966 edition of the Michiana Executive Journal featuring her work and life with the girls,she was described as "a gentle, soft-spoken person who exudes a quiet dignity and a friendly, if reserved personal manner." She definitely felt respect from the public. The public seemed to be enraged against Adam Portland and the legal system's carelessness, which led to Lana's murder.

The days became filled with handling life and death and raising two very active, intelligent girls. The notoriety of the case made every detail of the murder and trial everyday news. Lee received requests for interviews from every form of media: magazines, newspapers, radio, and television. Articles on the murder appeared everywhere. Following the airing of her interview on ABC's "20/20," which she felt was one of her best interviews, she received a call from a well-known journalist, Raymond Narsey. He told her that he was an author and was impressed with the way she handled the interview and suggested a book. She tabled that by placing his name, address, and phone number in her directory while she attended to more pressing issues.

Several years later, Lee put together some videos of Lana's murder and trial, as well as documentation of the work she had been doing on behalf of battered women, and sent it to Raymond Narsey and expressed interest in a book. She waited. Some time much later, she was informed by phone that he was busy working on other things. Soon she began to hear about a movie from the people at the women's shelter where Lana had worked. They believed it to be about Lana and Lee. Lee later heard about a movie called *In Honor Of Wanda*. She wondered if this could possibly have been based on the information she had naively provided to Raymond Narsey, but which she had not had copyrighted. She never saw the film the people at the women's shelter spoke of, nor did she have any time to pursue the issue.

When Lee began speaking publicly about Lana's story, she spoke to small, local groups in private homes. Later, she began to speak to larger gatherings in public venues. Almost every social and civic group wanted to hear the story. Then she began receiving calls from national documentary and news programs. She appeared on *The Oprah Winfrey* show, *48 Hours*, and *The Justice Files*. Local and national domestic violence and various women's organizations such as the National Coalition On Domestic Violence, the National Organization Of Women, directors of shelters, etc. asked Lee to speak at conferences. She traveled four states, taking with her the message of the thousands of battered women who had no voice of their own. She never solicited a speaking engagement, nor did she accept personal payment. Lee began to establish a reputation for credibility and bravery. People would come up to her in the street and say; "Don't ever stop doing what you're doing. We believe what you tell us; politicians just tell us what they want us to hear." She and the girls were well-known and Lee could feel the empathy of the community and surrounding areas in their cards, letters, and special actions, such as the establishment of a local trust fund for the girls.

At the same time, Lee was asked to run for local office. She declined. She knew that her daughter's murder could not be a political issue—it was a humanitarian issue. Besides, she was determined that politicians would use her no more than she would use them. Lee was working part-time and asked for and received permission from her employer to grant interviews in her office. In the first year, there were countless interviews granted to magazine reporters as well as the proposal of a book and movie. Articles appeared in magazines and papers across the nation. One article quoted a female attorney who asked, "What did she expect? She should have had a gun."

The fact is that Lana did have a permit and gun, but she could hardly leave a gun around with two children in the home. Furthermore, one cannot live their life sitting on the sofa with a loaded gun in hand. Upon reading this, one of Lee's friends blurted out: "Do these people think that the perpetrator is going to call and inform the victim of their estimated arrival time?" No. They stalk, plan, and use the element of surprise, kicking in doors or breaking out windows. Lee immediately felt that this comment had to come from someone with no experience with domestic violence. Lee consistently turned down any speaking requests that might portray any element of tawdriness or pettiness. There was no financial remuneration for any of the speaking engagements, as some people believed. Sometimes she traveled to the studio, and sometimes the interviewer and film crew flew in.

One of the things she learned was that in spite of the message you might want to get across, he who holds the microphone and has editing power is going to portray the story his or her way. When there was a proposal for her to appear on one of the nation's most famous talk shows, *The Oprah Winfrey Show,* she was assured that she would be given time to express her thoughts on how to remedy the situation, but when the program aired, the commentary from the other members of the panel and the gory details of the murders took precedence. Her sister had traveled to the studio with her and was seated in the audience. When the cameras stopped rolling, they looked at each other and simply shook their heads in disappointment and agreement..

CHAPTER 3: The Trial

Pre-Trial Preparations

Prior to the trial of this notorious murder case, there were many changes in terms of trial locations and judges. It was finally determined by those in charge that the trial would be held in St. James County, where the murder had occurred. The judge and jurors would come from Starke County, Indiana. That selection became noteworthy when the vehicle transporting the jurors was robbed while the jurors were dining at a restaurant along the route to Marietta. There were, of course, rumors that Adam Portland's cohorts had arranged this. A titillating suggestion, but Lee did not believe it.

Those were not the only rumors. During Adam's incarceration at the Marietta jail, he gave an interview to a local reporter. In that interview he told the reporter that the only reason he was in jail and that the state would ask for the death penalty was to forever silence him about an affair between the prosecutor and Lana. It was so typical of him to conjure up reasons to hold someone else responsible for his crimes. He had gotten away with so much for so long and he couldn't believe that he didn't have good reason to do what he did. Everything always had to be someone else's fault.

Then there were rumors about Lee. Because she was in the news so often, people exchanged Lana's and her names. While having dinner with friends one evening, Lee was asked if she had heard the rumors. Thinking that they meant the rumor about Lana and the prosecutor, she answered affirmatively. But the rumor was about *her* having an affair with the prosecutor. She laughed and said that she was flattered. The prosecutor was a good-looking man. She then mentioned it laughingly to several acquaintances and was shocked when they replied that they had heard it, but had told the informant that Lee was not the type of person to do that. It wasn't so funny after a while. But she finally came to the decision that people, being human, would continue. There was no way to control that and she could only steadfastly remain the person she knew she was.

The Trial

The girls had to testify in the murder case against their father. Despite Lee's requests for a video-only testimony, she was informed that the girls would need to appear in person because of another recent trial where the case was lost because the accused was not allowed to face the accuser. She received permission from the mother of one of the girls' playmates to have her daughter participate in practice sessions with the girls. They practiced walking through the underground tunnel from the prosecutor's office to the courthouse. The girls sat in the judge's chair and the witness chair. They saw where Daddy would be sitting and understood that he might have a mean look on his face.

Because so much national media had focused on the event and so much public animosity against Adam Portland prevailed, security at the courthouse was very tight. Everyone walked through metal detectors just outside the courtroom. Each morning of the trial, the girls' minister, Jack Smyth, or their assistant pastor, Dan Louterback, picked up Lee and the girls. Dan later became a foster-grandfather and a positive male role model to the girls. Many days passed while they waited their respective turns to testify.

A news photographer took one of the infamous photos of Adam during the trial, outside the courtroom. It showed him dressed in his three-piece suit, smiling arrogantly, with a cigarette dangling from his lip. Lee had been told that the defense attorney was Stan McQueen, an experienced death penalty attorney. Representatives of the prosecuting attorney's office instructed Lee that part of the defense's tactic would be to unnerve and anger her. That was just standard practice among attorneys attempting to discredit a witness. It would be the defense of "Bitch: like mother, like daughter." This would supposedly give more justification for the murder.

At first, Adam's attorney tried to establish some minor differences in Lee's statements to the police immediately following the murder, such as how many times Adam and Lana had separated. When Lee apologized for being confused because it was immediately following Lana's murder, he backed off. He then tried to ask her questions that were supposed to be answered with a simple yes or no and could therefore be misleading. Instead of yes or no, Lee responded to these questions with "some." The judge asked if she wanted the question repeated. She answered in the affirmative and again her response was "some." Knowing that the public, and probably the jury would be on her side, he changed tactics and made short work of her testimony.

Lee was not allowed in the courtroom while the girls were testifying because court officials said that she might influence them. She had no need to—they were there when the murder was committed. She was barred from the courtroom during all parts of the trial except for her direct testimony. Thus she was spared the crime scene photos and attacks on her daughter in the defense of the murderer, and she knew little of the testimony. She heard from others that three prisoners who knew Adam in jail testified of his proud retelling of the success of Lana's murder. She had a glimpse of the three men in orange jumpsuits, shackled and handcuffed, as they were led into the courtroom.

Alicia's testimony meant little because she was shy and not very responsive.

Brittany testified that Daddy had broken in the back door, that he had a "big stick" under his coat, and that he was "growling."

A tactic employed by the defense attorney did little to improve his case when he asked Brittany if she loved her daddy. To ask that question of a ten-year-old facing the man who killed her mother did not sit well with many.

The family also had to deal with alleged charges published that Lana was involved with drugs and other criminal activity. In a capital murder case, the defense can slander and make any charges they wish without having to prove the allegations. This is allowed because it is a "special situation" (i.e., a murder with death penalty invoked). So Adam Portland was not only able to brutally murder Lana in a public street, but now he was also able to heap additional abuse in the form of slander on her through his attorney.

The judge had decided that the trial would be over in two weeks. And so it was.

The verdict was guilty, and Adam Portland was sentenced to the death penalty. There were the expected throngs of reporters and cameras at the trial and penalty phase hearing. Photographs in the papers showed Adam dispassionate and smirking ever so slightly. Lee had not attended the penalty phase of the trial. Upon hearing the death penalty decision, she was not surprised, nor was she elated. She knew that it would not ease the pain of Lana's loss and that Adam would get to live many more years on the planet, unlike Lana. While Adam's rights would be protected for the rest of his life, the family would be left to deal with the aftermath for the rest of their lives. That was in 1990. Although the insanity plea had been struck down—eyewitnesses had testified, and Adam had not denied the crime—it took fifteen years before his sentence was carried out.

One day several years after the murder, Lee opened her front door to find one of Adam's post conviction attorneys on the steps. He asked her if Adam had to die. She replied, "I did not make that judgment," and closed the door. He, as well as many other legal representatives, continued working on Adam's defense until the end, all at taxpayer expense. When talking with local reporters, they would sometimes ask Lee why she hadn't been at a particular hearing on Adam's case. She could only respond: "What hearing?" She had not even been notified. Perhaps that was a blessing in disguise because at each hearing Lee attended, the defense attorneys would bring up the "she was a bitch" defense.

Lee would cringe whenever a murder trial came to a close with the guilty verdict, and she would read about the victim's relatives who said, "Now, justice has been served."

Oh, no. That is far from the truth. The verdict is just the starting point for most criminals and their attorneys. In letters to the governor and attorney general fifteen years after Lana's murder, Lee asked, "At what point does the legal system become immoral in denying the victim's rights?"

On the Death Penalty

As the mother of a brutally murdered victim, Lee always read with interest the views of others on the death penalty. Several times she confronted Notre Dame law professors (in print) on this issue. Lee would smile as she questioned, "How much can a Notre Dame law professor know about the realities of the legal system with his view from the library?"

Henry David Thoreau wrote in his *Journal, February 19, 1841* "*A truly good book teaches me better than to read it. I must lay it down and commence living on its hint....What I began by reading I must finish by acting."* Realities must be factored into ideology.

The opinions of lawyers sometimes propagate fees. When they refer to the bankruptcy of the death sentence, the bankruptcy really comes from the continued ability for the murderer to employ attorneys and make constant pleas at the taxpayers' expense.

The death penalty was not a deterrent for Adam Portland because he knew that the average length of time received as punishment for murder, as he intimated to Lee, is eight years. What kind of framework for punishment have we given prospective murderers like him? How could the death penalty be a deterrent when it has not often been used because it paves the way for many years of taxpayer-funded assistance, in addition to all the money spent to bring the criminal to trial and justice? How can it be a deterrent if it's not employed in a timely fashion?

The death penalty trial is one that allows the defense special permission to defame and slander the victim at trial without having to prove the accusations. It means year after year of pleas and trials at the family's emotional expense, all on the taxpayers' dime. Lee's view on the death penalty was based on a twenty-year interaction with the victim, the murderer, and the legal system. Every time a criminal is not made to suffer the consequences of his actions, he is reinforced.

While some people feel that taking a life is wrong, what message is being sent to the murderer-to-be? There is what Lee came to call the "warm and fuzzy Christianity" ethic. It wants to save a life. It makes people feel good. What we don't need is to feel good. What we need is the truth.

We should be investigating and employing what is in the best interest of society. That means removing anything sectarian on the issue. One argument for the abolishment of the death penalty is, "this is not a sectarian teaching, but an affirmation that the state is not God."

Lee would contend that neither is God the state. The "state" is a concept created by man. Social issues can only be resolved by seeing ourselves as part of something larger, as a society. That insight cannot be biased by anything sectarian. What is not recognized and cannot be calculated is the harm done to society when good people embrace bad causes. This feeds into the system whereby those promoting the bottom line, profit, are used. We had Monica Lewinsky for Jenny Craig, Benneton marketing T-shirts with death-row inmates on the front, lots of movies with "very nice, probably innocent" murderers who, not surprisingly, suddenly found God—all proof that anyone is somewhat redeemable for a profit. The fact that a seller would use the image of someone who allegedly committed a grave offense gives their persona some convoluted credence and visibility. The greatest profit is for the retailer, unless the ploy backfires.

By glorifying and representing those who are character-deficient, we move in direct opposition to what is best for our society. We remove accountability and the rights of victims. While it is known that timely use of an employed death penalty would not necessarily prevent all murders, Lee could say with 99 percent certainty that it would have in Adam's case ... there was no one who valued his own skin the way he did. He requested that he be turned in after the murder by an officer he was familiar with. He also requested that he be turned into a police department where he felt he had friends on the force and so would be assured that he wasn't beaten by other inmates.

Nowadays, with the huge implications of DNA evidence to prevent mistakes, the death penalty could be used with more conviction, but it has fallen out of favor. One of the reasons is the cost. But why should it cost more to carry out the death penalty than to provide shelter, food, medical and dental care, and all the necessities of life to a convicted murderer until his death? The answer is the high cost of fifteen to twenty years of legal defenses. The preparations for a death penalty trial are exhaustive and they need to be able to withstand year after year of appeals.

While Lee believed in God and Christian principles, she felt that the first consideration should be the obligation to society—not what makes a person feel good or brings in money. If all those who work on behalf of those who consciously chose to murder another human being would take the time to find out that criminals have a limitless fund at their disposal with expenses being paid by taxpayers, they might think differently. If they knew the crying need of victims for the same rights, privileges and protections the criminals have, they might think differently. Lee knew, Lana knew ...

CHAPTER 4:
The Guardianship

Fight for Guardianship

A few days after Lana's murder, Lee sat slumped over the conference table in the estate attorney's office. Her head was lying on her outstretched arms. She had been given immediate temporary custody of the girls and she hadn't expected anything to change before it became permanent. But Adam Portland was demanding a custody hearing. How could this be? How could the law ask her to face the man who had, just a few short days ago, murdered her daughter? Because he was the biological father and those were his rights under "the law?" Overwhelming feelings of disgust, fear, and dread filled her. She pleaded with the attorney asking, "How can they expect me to do this? Is there never any compassion for victims in the law?"

"No", he answered coolly. "And, besides, you're his next victim."

The days were a blur of media invasion and the integration of the lives of Lana's two children with hers. Ten-year old Brittany had the fair coloring, blonde hair, and blue eyes of her father. Alicia, the four-year old, had the olive complexion, dark hair and brown eyes of her mother. They were beautiful, intelligent children. Lee found her only relief by saving her screams and fist-poundings for times when the girls were in school. She would lie in bed and remember that from the birth of her first child in her nightly prayers, the only thing she had asked of God was to not let anything bad happen to her children. First it had been Marty, now Lana. There would be no more nightly prayers. While she attended church and believed in God, she no longer believed in divine intervention.

Yet, she did pray for guidance and wisdom for the girls' future. What would be best for them? What could she do? When Lee was only eleven years old, her own mother had died suddenly, leaving her the oldest girl in a farm family where conveniences such as indoor plumbing, hot water, and automatic washers and dryers were non-existent. There had been four children ranging in ages from four to thirteen, and she had to assume responsibility overnight. Then there was her own family. Lee had grown up and matured in the 1950s and had that era's dream career of women—all she wanted to be was a successful wife and mother and to raise happy and healthy children.

Now, here she was, divorced, with two of her children dead—and two grandchildren who needed her. She had initiated the divorce, and she remembered that when she left to move into a vacant rental house she and her husband had owned, there had been newspapers on the windows and cockroaches in the cupboards. But she had wanted to get down on her knees and thank God for the return of her dignity. Her life after the divorce became a happy one with a good job that she liked, independence, and a satisfying social and church life.

Lee knew that the ideal situation for the girls would be in a good, two-parent family. Lee had had that family structure and she felt that it was the best possible situation if both parents were competent, able, and willing. Even though her mother had died when she was young, she had felt her influence and knew that children needed both a mother and father. The closest two-parent family meant her son, Mason, and daughter-in-law, Mara. Her instincts caused her gut fear. Lee had seen her daughter-in-law set out to break the close relationship she had with her first-born son. She knew of Mara's emotional instability and the history of rescue and abandonment within her family. She had seen her cold, domineering nature, the hands that pushed children away when they came for reassurance. She had observed Mara, with horror, as she jerked her own children by the hair and slapped them across their faces. Mara's character could be read in her face with its coarse, sallow-skinned features. The small, dark-rimmed, deep set eyes, narrowed with sarcasm, and glittering with hardness. The narrow lips set in a perpetual downward turn at the corners, her face framed in a cap of jet-black hair. She was employed as a matron at a nearby women's detention center. Lee felt that she knew how long the guardianship would last and what her grandchildren would be subjected to. She knew that a parent must be a positive, consistent presence. Being a parent is what you do, not what you promise. She knew what kind of role model Mara would be. Lee also knew that the maternal bond was hers and Lana's, and she had to resume the role. She could show the girls how to overcome adversity, not allowing them to be treated as "poor little girls," but as girls who could live a good life and grow to become happy and productive members of society.

The date of the guardianship hearing was fast approaching. It was just weeks after Lana's death. Lee prayed for strength and wore a little silver ring of Lana's on her finger, as if it were a part of Lana fortifying her. The time was now. The attorneys for the estate and the recently appointed guardianship attorney were there and the girls' father was there with his court-appointed attorney. Lee noticed that Adam's attorney sat with his chair slightly drawn away from Adam, as if trying to distance himself from him.

Adam had a yellow legal pad in front of him. His head was down and he was busily writing, pausing only now and then to hold whispered conferences with his attorney. He was not wearing prison garb; the state had dressed him as befits one of their own in a suit and tie, lending him the appearance of a reputable person. That was another one of his rights.

Lee thought of this handsome, charming man who had washed dishes in her kitchen, complimented her cooking, and viciously murdered her defenseless daughter. Now here he was, asserting his right to say where his daughters were to go. She remembered the times he had used them as pawns, kidnapping them and holding them hostage to get his way. It was always the same thing—Lana was not to divorce him and was to drop the rape charges against him. If beating, harassment, intimidation, and rape didn't work, then the children were kidnapped.

Lee's ex-husband, Vincente, also attended the guardianship hearing. Mason and Mara chose not to attend. Adam requested that the girls go to his brother and sister-in-law in South Carolina—people the girls had seen perhaps a handful of times in their lives. They were not present but represented by a three-page letter written on yellow legal paper by someone alleging to be the brother's pastor.

When it came time for Lee to take the stand, Adam's lawyer asked, "Ms. Bordolos, didn't you state to the media that you thought you were too old to take care of the children?"

Lee almost laughed out loud. That statement seemed unbelievably ridiculous. She was healthy, in her early fifties, and felt capable of any trial set before her. Even if the idea had occurred to her, she certainly wouldn't have publicly admitted to being too old!

On the stand, she affirmed that the girls had, over the years, spent a lot of time with her. They were very close and loved her. She affirmed that they had been living with her since Lana's murder, that they were enrolled in the same school they had always attended, were also enrolled in Sunday school, and were going to summer camp that year. The bottom line came when the attorney asked her why the girls had spent so much time with her over the years, especially the past few. The answer was obvious—for shelter and comfort.

Lee's ex-husband, Vincente, testified that she was the best person to care for the children. He stated that they had spent much time with her, and also that Lee disciplined them properly when necessary. A local newspaper account quoted his "pledge of emotional and financial support." How convoluted that statement would become in the years ahead, Lee could not have imagined. Vincente would come to use her guardianship and the children's trust as a means of payback for their divorce, which he had not wanted. Preceding the divorce and forever after, Lee would continue to wonder which he would miss more—her and her services, or her share of the community property.

The judge awarded guardianship to her and she left the courtroom.

Later that day, Lee visited her son and daughter-in-law. Mara was not there and Mason treated her coldly. She tried to feel him out. Why was he treating her this way?

Mason made one terse statement, "You and Dad won."

Lee was baffled. Had Mason and Mara put this on the level of a competition? They had not filed for guardianship and were not in the courtroom during the proceedings, which was their choice. Lee had previously told Mason and Mara that she intended to leave her job to take full-time care of the girls, which was something they would surely need. Mason and Mara's financial situation would not allow them to add another two children to the two they already had.

Lee couldn't tell them the real reason she didn't think they should have guardianship of the girls: Mara. She did not have either the staying power or the proper motivation. Lee had seen the malevolence in Mara's face. Mara claimed to have promised Lana that if anything happened to her, she and Mason would take the girls. Yet Lana had told Lee, only months before her death, that Mara had refused to care for the girls while she was in class and at work because she couldn't pay Mara the rate she requested.

Lee had often seen Mara at the bedside of a sick or dying person, full of the "let me in on the tragedy" attitude. She had seen a generational tendency in Mara's family to take in relatives or friends in trouble, but when it became tiring or inconvenient, they threw them out. The girls were not puppies to be discarded when they wet the rug, or to be used for temporary glorification and then discarded. The girls needed a lifetime commitment come hell or high water. Vincente and Mara would do everything in their power to see that Lee got both hell and high water during the entire course of the guardianship.

On a subsequent visit to Mason and Mara's, Mara shouted at Lee as she went out the door, "When you've lost your last child, you'll know what you've done!"

Financial Issues: Getting the Trust

Lee wanted the girls to be physically, emotionally, spiritually, and financially taken care of. When she decided to devote herself to the task, she divested herself of any future financial security. She would be over sixty years old when Alicia turned eighteen—not old enough for Social Security assistance or Medicare health insurance. Fortunately, she had two small rental properties, and the girls would be receiving social security. But in order to raise them the way Lana would want, Lee would need more money, especially when it came to their college expenses.

Many had suggested a suit against the Department of Corrections and the State of Indiana. When Adam was originally incarcerated, both Lana and the County Prosecutor's office had requested that she be notified if Adam were ever released from prison for any reason, since he had promised to kill her and had made previous attempts on her life. No one notified Lana on the day he was released, and she was murdered.

Lee made an appointment to visit an attorney regarding the matter. The attorney's attitude was not encouraging, saying that the case could be tied up in the courts for years, and it would be doubtful that it would pay off. He said it was too late for justice for Lana.

She left his office, but Lee was undaunted and found another firm—a father and son team with a high success rate in wrongful death and injury claims. The father did not seem very interested, but the son did, and he set the process in motion.

The eventual outcome was a settlement from the state that brought the girls three times the cap, or limit of $300,000 for wrongful death in the state of Indiana. The attorney had filed three separate claims: one on behalf of Lana's estate and two for each of the girls. As a public relations gesture, he took only 10 percent of the $900,000. The normal attorney fee would have been one third of the settlement money received. The money went directly into a bank trust and was controlled by trust officers.

Some people asked, "Is that all a life is worth?" while others whispered furtively, "Well, it is taxpayer money, you know." Some were concerned about spending taxpayer money and others felt that the girls had received too little.

Defending the Trust Against Others

It was now time to find a good home for the new family. Lee's background in real estate directed her to a condo in a good school district and a good resale area. A single woman in her fifties raising two girls and working on behalf of battered women would have little strength for heavy yard work and home maintenance. The home was nice enough that the girls could be proud of it, but not so opulent that they couldn't aspire to better. It was also something she could afford to buy an interest in and provide her share of maintenance costs. Although the trust made provisions for them for housing, she instinctively knew better than to live long-term in a home solely owned by the girls' trust. She had visions of a rebellious teen granddaughter saying, "This is my house and I'll do what I want with it."

Lee purchased a share substantial enough that it would not be easy to be displaced, and she would pay her share of the maintenance and utilities. They closed the sale at the bank, but there would be no housewarming party. Her ex-husband, who was on file as an "interested party," brought suit against Lee because he hadn't been consulted during the transaction and was not asked to be at the closing. Even though he had no responsibilities or money invested, his ego got in the way.

The matter was taken to court and no improprieties were found. This was the beginning of a series of lawsuits that would drain thousands upon thousands of dollars from the girls' trust over the next twelve years—all in defense of frivolous charges and slander. A simple internet word search shows the legal definition of an interested party as an: *"Entity who has a recognizable stake in the outcome of a matter before a court, but may not be directly involved in the litigation process."*

It is possible to destroy trust with nothing more than insinuation and lies. Lee once asked Vincente the question, "If you really love the girls, how can you destroy their trust in the only person who's been there for them all their lives, who is their support and parent and how will they feel when they find out the truth?"

He replied with silence. Lee likened it to Lana's situation, where the law gave the abuser the freedom to continually confront and attack, but never gave her the freedom to fight back.

Thus, the money she put in place for the girls and their future would be used incessantly to harass her through the courts. It was no surprise to anyone that not one instance of wrongdoing was ever found, but going through the courts gave the charges an air of undeserved credibility. To twist children's minds is reprehensible enough, but to use their own money to do it is abhorrent.

One of the greatest revelations she would have much later regarded the influence of the guardianship attorney. While Lee was being subjected to constant harassment through the courts by "interested parties," Lee asked if she could get some freedom from these constant assaults by moving a thousand miles away. The attorney hesitated for a moment and then replied, "No."

Lee would be left to wonder about the attorney's motivation. Lee really didn't think it was money, but considering the countless thousands of dollars spent in her defense of Vincente's charges, Lee began to question the attorney's reply. Perhaps he didn't know, as she knew in her heart, that the corruption of the girls and many of the court hearings would have been almost impossible from that distance. One thing was certain—Lee's emotional havoc was work for the attorney and the accountant. The difference was that their reward was a paid invoice from the girls' trust, while hers was more emotional abuse. She often thought of finding a legislator who would sponsor a bill for the protection of guardians and trust funds. The number of times the guardian could be harassed seemed to be limitless. This would be a good place for the "three strikes and you're out" rule, placing a limit on the number of times a guardian could be unsuccessfully charged and taken to court by the same individual.

Lee and the girls soon settled into their lifestyle—the girls attended school and were involved in a multitude of social, physical, and church activities, while Lee structured and accommodated their lives. It was important for her to be there for them. She knew that they were hungry for security, and one of her main goals in life was to fill that need. Lee recalled a school function of Brittany's shortly after Lana's death. When she arrived and took her place with the other parents in the gym, she could see Brittany's beautiful little face, almost desperately scanning the crowd for her. While in church, Brittany would sit up tight against her as though afraid of separation.

Lee's employer, Star Staffing Associates, was very generous with her and allowed Lee to work part-time so that she could accommodate the girls' schedules. She carried a phone with her at all times so that the girls would have instant access to her. One day, hurrying home from her job in order to be there the moment Brittany got out of school, she ran a stop sign and was involved in an accident. When the police arrived on the scene, she made it the first order of business for them to contact the school and get the message to Brittany.

Over the next several years, Lee's main preoccupation was being there for her granddaughters, and this gave her a sense of completion. She continued to see that they were in good schools and had a good home to bring friends to. Lee took the girls on hundreds of shopping trips. They participated in school and church activities, after-school and weekend and evening lessons including ballet, gymnastics, Little League, cheerleading, summer camps, and any other they wanted to participate in. Lee took them to the orthodontist, on vacations, and to church activities. She attempted to expose them to a broad spectrum of art, theatre, and travel. Even prior to Lana's murder, Lee had loved the girls' visits—their shopping trips, and decorating and arranging birthday parties for them. She had always loved them so much, and her pride in them and in the work she did for them, especially now, gave her life meaning.

Both the girls were outgoing to the point that they felt they could do anything. Each activity warranted its own apparel and schedule. Sometimes Lee fell asleep in the car, waiting to pick them up. It was not all fun and games.

Lee wanted to instill a good work ethic in her granddaughters, trust fund notwithstanding—they would need that later. The trust could disappear quickly, despite the built-in spendthrift clause. Consequently, the girls found work delivering papers or waitressing. There was no car waiting for them when they turned sixteen unless they could afford to pay for it and the related expenses. Lee knew full well that when the girls would resent this in the short term, but she was looking out for their futures. They could always complain to the do-nothings and get sympathy and confirmation that Grandma was mean.

Lee promised the girls that they would go away for a few months after the trial was over, so she made arrangements to rent a small place in Florida. They visited the popular tourist attractions and went to the movies and roller-skating. It turned out to be an expensive vacation for Lee. While there, she received a "Dear Joan" letter from the man she had been dating, and when they returned to Indiana, her ex-husband, Vincente, was waiting with another court date. He was protesting that she had spent too much of the trust money on the vacation—approximately $4,000 for two months. She could prove that she had paid her share of the vacation, but he still had to throw his weight around. After all, he hadn't been consulted or asked to go along.

At the hearing, the judge asked Vincente how much money the girls had. Vincente seemed confused and replied, "Huh?"

The judge repeated: "How much money do they have?"

When the reply came back, "Almost a million dollars," the judge's response was, "And you would deny them this vacation?"

The courts understood early on what her ex-husband was all about. Judges often admonished him to stop fighting an old divorce in the courtroom, but no one prevented him from doing it repeatedly over the years.

Corruption of the Girls

At home, something strange was happening. Brittany, who had always talked about how mean Aunt Mara was and how poorly she treated Uncle Mason, now seemed to want to spend time there. Lee welcomed this since Mara had refused to have anything to do with the girls for almost a year after Lana's death, punishing them for Lee's guardianship. But the girls would come home from those visits in a brooding and argumentative state.

On one occasion, Brittany told her, "All you do is hand out the state's money."Lee's response to these attacks was also strange. She was so concerned about their emotional well-being and wanting them to think they had nice relatives and an allied family that she said next to nothing in her own defense. No indignity, no telling them that their trust had come about solely through her efforts, no telling them of her sacrifices and total devotion to their well-being. She was sure they would know all this as they grew up. The counselor she had been seeing about the problem with Mara and Vincente had advised her, "Don't get into pissing contests with them; they're better pissers."

As Lee would realize later, the long-term dripping of venom and lies would eventually filter through to the girls.

Lee asked for a family counseling session with Mara and her son with a trained and accredited professional. Five minutes into the session, Mara got up and walked out. With her customary dignity and tact, she stated flatly, "I can't handle this shit."

Her son, Mason, the son who had always been first with gifts and Mother's Day cards, the happy and affectionate son, followed his wife out. It was Mara's style to scheme, plot, direct, construct her scapegoat and then remove herself from any accountability. Mason had been a happy, loving son at eighteen. He had had exceptional musical talent with plans for further study. Then at nineteen, he met an older, tougher woman. The way that Mara dominated and manipulated him shows that the more naïve partner will eventually give in. In order to go along with what they know is wrong, they will accept and participate in their partner's behavior in order to justify a situation they are unable to change.

When she recounted her experience in the family counselor's office to her ex-husband, his reply was, "That's between you and Mason."

The message from him was that whatever lashes came across her back, whether engineered by him or by others, were no more than she deserved. Lee was familiar with Vincente's capacity for maliciousness. She had long ago learned of the rumors he had spread after their separation. One was that he had tried to prevent Marty, the son they lost in an automobile accident, from using her car that night, but that Lee had overruled him. Another rumor was that Lee had "taken him so badly" in the divorce that he had to take in a female boarder because he needed the money. The same boarder was there twenty years later, in spite of Vincente's boast that he had more money than the mayor of Marietta.

Later on, Mara spread rumors that she had wanted family counseling, but that Lee had refused. Her campaign was not unlike

Adam's campaign with Lana—Mara's goal was to destroy Lee. Mara, she later found out, had called one of the same agencies that Adam had called on Lana, ones that deals with child abuse and neglect. Mara also went to the girls' schools and talked with their principals, spreading rumors about Lee. The greatest cruelty often wears the disguise of concern and kindness. This egotistical and noxious behavior was a way for Mara to damage someone she viewed as her rival.

Lee remembered how her family had tried to resist the onslaught of Mara's negativity. On Lee's birthday, Mason and his stepson brought her a birthday cake and tried to celebrate with her. Brittany was on break from college, telling Lee about Mara's phone calls to her while at school. She told Lee that the calls tore her up so much that her roommate soon refused to tell her when Aunt Mara called, and that she had lost three months of school. She was unable to do her school work and was seeing a counselor.

Mara   never considered in her denigration of Brittany's grandmother that one of the leading causes of death among teenagers is suicide. The Centers for Disease Control and Prevention report that suicide is the third leading cause of death, behind accidents and homicide, of people aged fifteen to twenty-four, according to the Web site www. teensuicidestatistics.com. Mara's heartless tirades occurred at the most vulnerable time of Brittany's life, as though she did not have enough to deal with emotionally.

Alicia, on the other hand, was not so easily poisoned. She was attending a school for grades seven thru twelve in Utah, as her scholastic counselor and advisor wanted her as far away as possible from her family. Within two weeks of Alicia's arrival, the school cut off all calls from Aunt Mara. They told Lee that those calls had been so damaging that it took them two weeks to get Alicia straightened out afterwards.

The family—Mara, Mason and Vincente—was also in a position to be the "good guys" and the girls' champions. They undermined anything that Lee had done for their long-term benefit. If Lee insisted on calling the parents at a party the girls might attend to make sure they were supervised, she was portrayed as untrusting. Of course, being children, they often enjoyed the sympathy and attention they received from the rest of the family. After one of Brittany's visits to her grandfather's home, she asked Lee: "Why is there a picture of the liquor bottles on the shelf in our garage on Grandpa's computer?" He had taken the picture one day when he was picking up the girls and added it to his inventory of incriminating evidence against Lee.

Both Vincente and Mara repeatedly told the girls, "Just wait 'till you're eighteen." Likewise, they told Lee: "Just wait 'till they're eighteen."

They coached the girls to rebel and encouraged them to buy anything they wanted through the trust. The rest of the family bought the girls with their own money, money Lee had provided for their futures.

One of the responsibilities of guardianship was the accounting of money. The attorney for the trust waited until two weeks before the first biennial accounting was due in probate court to notify Lee of that responsibility. At first Lee sought the advice of the estate attorney. He gave her some bad advice that co-mingled funds that could have proved problematic except for her strict record keeping. Her record keeping, receipts, spreadsheets and validation by a CPA were more than a probate judge was accustomed to receiving, according to the guardianship attorney. She called on an economist at the local university, but he couldn't help. She researched at the library, but she couldn't find any help or guidance. This was at a point in time before the lawsuit had gone forward. When the lawsuit was awarded, Lee installed more detailed financial tracking software on her computer and broke down their expenses into fourteen categories and prorated community expenses (ongoing expenses such as utilities, food, insurance, etc.) accordingly. The girls' personal expenses were documented, both with duplicate checks and receipts. She furnished a written itemization of each category, so as to allay any accounts of vagueness. She kept a monthly spreadsheet and retained the services of a CPA to prepare the report for probate at every two-year mark. The girls had their guardianship attorney and trust officer. The financial settlement from the state as a result of the lawsuit was made to the trust at a local bank. The monies invested and their earnings, as well as any disbursements, were controlled and recorded by the trust department of the bank.

At each accounting, Vincente would appear, swaggering in with his ruled legal pad. Besides dragging Lee into court for frivolous charges, Vincente always had a litany of complaints about her spending. One complaint was that that Lee had spent the vast sum of $42 for office supplies over a two-year period. Another $300 mattress and box spring dragged through two more accountings. At one of the accountings, Lee's ex-husband reported that she had three closets full of clothes, while the girls each had only a few outfits.

The old boy's club was already at work at the time of Lee's and the girls' pending home purchase of the condo. There was a meeting arranged with all the attorneys for the trust and the bank. She arrived early. Only one of the attorneys was there and his first remark to Lee was, "You know, Vincente said that you were moving into the condo with a man, and we can't have that."

Lee's mouth dropped open. She couldn't believe that they would automatically believe everything Vincente told them. The fact that it was not true did not anger her so much as their inevitable acceptance of anything he said to defame her. She had witnessed, firsthand, how attorneys fawned over her ex-husband. It was as though she was only a cute little blonde who could cook and clean for the girls. The extent of that old boys' network almost drove her to a nervous breakdown. She would hear comments from male family members that reinforced stereotypical attitudes about women: "I think that's a good arrangement. You can take care of the kids and Vincente can keep an eye on the money" Did they think that she couldn't do both when she was already tracking and providing proof of every penny disbursed? Did they think that she would misuse the money or might not keep track of it? These were hard things to bear, even though the remarks were made innocently.

The old boy's club took on a new and more forceful life when the trust changed hands and a new trust officer was installed. Lee's ex-husband began paying many visits to the newbie, Jack Robeson. The monthly budget for the girls had been established from documentation that Lee had provided the courts and the amount approved. The method of confirmation would be the biennial accounting, unless otherwise deemed necessary. Soon after Vincente's courtship of the bank trust officer, the bank started changing practices that had already been established and approved by the court. The guardianship attorney didn't seem much bothered by it, but it caused Lee great additional stress. She had returned to work part-time, and while she was out of town working on a temporary assignment of one week, the guardianship attorney called. He told Lee that Vincente wanted copies of her income taxes, a listing of all her speaking engagements (she never solicited speaking engagements or charged a fee), and that she was to give a deposition on these items. She had to leave her work in order to deal with this harassment. The purpose of a trust is to administer monies and follow court appointed directives. The bank should have known these directives and not allowed itself to be manipulated and directed by a vengeful ex-husband. The trust department, which succumbed to Vincente's manipulation, did a terrible disservice to Lee and indirectly, to the girls. A trust officer is not in the business of helping the guardian, but should at the very least know the court's decisions and adhere to them.

The strain of raising two teenagers, working part-time, and working on behalf of battered women was well within her capabilities, but the her ex-husband's unchallenged harassment was taking her over the top. She felt that she knew, on a small scale, how Lana felt, never knowing when or how the attacker would strike next. And, like Lana, the law didn't stop it.

At the same time, there were men making money from her misery. At additional expense, Lee was able to stop Vincente's unreasonable demands by asking for a deposition from him. Meanwhile, the bank was changing the practices and denying her the monies she needed to pay some of the girls' expenses, which had been approved by the courts. Even with documentation, they ignored her and she had to pay some of the expenses out of her own pocket. At first, the bank said to provide copies of utilities and other expenses. Then, they wanted the original statements—the same statements she would need for the probate accounting. When she submitted the originals to the bank, they delayed the payments and sometimes never returned the originals. All of this was caused by Vincente's manipulation of the trust officer.

The End of Guardianship

As soon as the girls reached their eighteenth birthdays, they were geared up for the freedom and money promised them as their due. They became Grandpa's girls and fell under his influence. He told them that he had made a promise to himself a long time ago to "take care of them." But he was starting now, after twelve years? During that twelve year period he saw them once or twice a month, usually to go out for dinner. At eighteen they each had new cars, a lovely apartment and nice furnishings. Grandma sold her china, crystal, one of her two rental properties and her interest in the condo and moved into pre-owned "manufactured housing." The girls could visit with their grandfather and tell him about their European vacations that the trust provided them. Mr. Bordolos had also of late become a world traveler They bought gifts with their trust money—not for Lee, but for those who tore them away from her. It was a good thing that she never expected any rewards for her act of love. She didn't blame the girls. They were being used as pawns, just as their father had used them.

Two years before her graduation from college, Brittany called Lee to tell her that she wanted no more contact with her. Lee had the respect and admiration from society at all levels, but not from those she loved most. She knew why, but that did not prevent her heart from breaking. Lee tried for four years to maintain contact with Brittany, sending expressions of love and remembrances of her special days. This was her firstborn, beautiful grandchild. She had provided her with all the good things in life and had seen to her every need and many of her wants. Thanks to Lee, Brittany had beautiful straight teeth, had attended one of the best prep schools in the state, and was attending one of the best colleges in the nation.

One evening while moving Alicia to a new school, Brittany called from Aunt Mara's home to rant and rage at Lee. While she made no specific accusations, Lee surmised that she was being convinced that her grandmother was taking advantage of the trust. One issue that she brought up was the fact that Lee was receiving assistance from the trust in the form of minimum wage based on a four-hour day. When Lee's employer no longer gave her part-time work and she was unable to take full-time work because of her duties to the girls, she received that compensation from the trust. It was one of the lowest points in her life, and if she had not had Alicia to deal with, she seriously would have contemplated suicide.

Years later, she would remember these events and be incredulous that she did not react violently. Was it because of the girls' position in the middle? Her sense of not wanting to stoop to the level of her attackers? The shock of her attackers' tactics? Or was she just too tired? Under Aunt Mara's tutelage and with Vincente's approval and enjoyment, Brittany chose to shun her grandmother, the worst punishment there is after physical torture and imprisonment. Brittany was her firstborn grandchild. Lee loved her fiercely, and Brittany's refusal to acknowledge her led to endless hours of grief and many sleepless nights spent on her computer, talking to her in print. Mara had begun the practice of shunning Lee soon after she became the girls' guardian. She returned her Christmas gifts and refused her attempts at family counseling and weekly dinners. Mara took over family traditions that Lee had established, taking them on as her own. When the girls would have a birthday party, Mara would have a private one for them before Lee did, stealing the first blush of excitement. Then, she refused to come to the parties Lee gave for them. Of course, Mason followed suit. Lee did not blame the girls so much. They were naive and must have thought, "If all these people love me, why would they lie?"

With persistence, young minds can be twisted, especially if someone is holding out a carrot with no stick. Brittany's graduation from one of the most prestigious universities in the country was a source of both pride and pain for Lee. Lee was installed in her little home in Florida when she received the printed invitation. Since there had been no communication with Brittany, she was surprised to receive the invitation. Lee wanted so much to be a part of the life she had helped to create for Brittany. She excitedly spent twelve hours traveling, including an overnight bus trip, often changing seat partners as the bus stopped numerous times. She arrived at the Atlanta bus station at 5:30 AM on Mother's Day and sat for three hours, waiting to be picked up. As she waited, her thoughts returned to another Mother's Day, when she and Lana and the girls were hiding from Adam in an off-the-road motel.

Before the graduation ceremony on the college campus began, Lee was left to wander alone among the guests of other graduates. She walked the fringe areas of the ceremony site like an interloper, wondering if her bleeding heart would show stains on her dress. She looked around the lawn to see if there were stones she could use to plug the holes, but there were none. She wanted to will herself to die, but knew that she mustn't because no one would know who she was—or care.

During the ceremony, Lee sat by herself in the audience, far from the proceedings. No doubt, Vincente and his lady friend occupied the places of honor reserved for parents. Lee did not even think about how she had made the trust possible, how she had made it possible for Brittany to attend the best prep schools, how she had taken Brittany on her college visits, how she installed Brittany in university life, and how she was responsible, along with Lana, for the person Brittany had become. She wanted to concentrate on her pride in Brittany. When Brittany arrived at the rear of the campus on her grandfather's arm, there was a smug look was on Vincente's face, as if he had stolen the prize. Yet Lee did not blame Brittany.

The school Alicia attended required Lee's attendance every three months for a week to ten days at a time. The trips involved three separate airplane flights, a rental car, and a seventy-mile trip through the mountains. Once there, Lee met with counselors and attended conferences and special programs. Some programs were for parents only and others were for both parents and children.

One such wilderness program required that Lee spend a night in the desert. It was New Year's Eve, and Lee and Alicia were in a solo campsite that had Alicia had set up. Lee broke ice in a creek and they drank water that they had treated with iodine. They cooked over a campfire Alicia made—Lee chopped onions on a split log.

Lee always viewed these trips as a privilege and a badge of honor. Alicia was a beautiful young woman, her granddaughter, and one of the loves of her life. Lee could not work a full-time job; no employer would give her the ten days every three months she needed to be there for the parental involvement programs. Lee's most important job was to be there for Alicia. And Lee and Alicia formed a strong bond, in spite of everything and everyone.

While Alicia was in school in Utah, Vincente and Mara circulated rumors that Lee had rid herself of her granddaughter by placing her in a lock-down school in the wilderness. Her grandfather scheduled a hearing, necessitating Alicia's leave from school. The judge found a well-dressed, poised, articulate, and attractive young woman who had good grades and a concise plan for her future. Her grandfather, the person who had made the charges and instigated the hearing, did not even have the courtesy to show up.

The judge asked the trust officer if he had heard from Mr. Bordolos. As he started to reply, the judge tersely stated, "I'm really not interested in anything Mr. Bordolos has to say."

During the time of Lee's guardianship, there were many men interested in dating her, but men over fifty who would be willing to commit to raising children at this stage in life were as scarce as the proverbial hen's teeth. Lee's traditional values would not allow her to cohabitate with a man while raising two young girls. At one point, Lee did marry. It was several years after she took guardianship, but the marriage lasted only a year. Soon after Lee and her new husband married, Vincente took her to court, protesting that Lee's new husband was renting out his own home while living with Lee and the children. Her new husband had, in fact, made the move at Lee's request. She did not want to relocate the girls. Vincente's complaint was, as usual, thrown out of court, but this constant harassment, coupled with the challenges of raising two children was just too much for someone who did not have the bond and commitment that Lee did. As hard as the divorce was on Lee, she had been independent for a long time. She had also suffered the loss of two children. What was this in comparison?

At the next biennial accounting, her ex-husband came with his usual yellow legal tablet filled with petty insinuations and charges. By this time, Vincente had so entrenched himself into the trust that he actually was seated at counsel table with the trust officer. The girls' guardianship attorney was as enraged as Lee was by the flagrant display of the old boy's club and did what he could to break it up, but Vincente kept his seat. This was the first time in the twelve years of the guardianship that she had been treated so contemptuously by the trust.

Mara was present, along with her brother and cousin. She had written a rambling eight-page letter denigrating Lee and had sent it to the judge. When he asked her to read it, she quickly replied, "I'm just a bystander."

The judge replied indignantly, "Well, you wrote it." Mara refused.

Brittany was on hand and the judge reminded her that the services of the guardianship attorney and the accountant were $200 per hour each, and she might want to have a say in how her money was spent. He was trying to alert her to the fact that the trust money was being squandered. Although she was seated on the same side of the courtroom as her grandmother, but not alongside her, Brittany replied: "I'm not on anyone's side, I just want to know what's happening with the money." Although both the guardianship attorney and the CPA talked with her following the hearing and encouraged her to come to them with any questions, she did not. It was easier to let things go and trust that her grandfather was representing her interests.

Nothing changed. The attacks continued under the guise of love. The family had Brittany's head in a vise. Torn between her grandmother and the rest of the family, Brittany was confused by the incessant slander against Lee. Dealing with these complications while trying to succeed in college led Brittany down the path of least resistance, the same path that her uncle Mason had taken.

At the time of her eighteenth birthday, Alicia decided that she would go to live with her sister and attend college in Georgia. After affirming her wishes many times, Lee decided to sell her furniture and put their home on the market. She then moved her things to her new home in Florida. Surprisingly, Alicia then did a complete reversal and decided to stay in the now nearly-empty condo. Alicia was now of legal age, and Lee could do nothing about it. Thus the do-nothings and whisperers were able to encourage her wishes and spread the rumor that Lee had dumped her eighteen-year-old granddaughter and left her alone and moved out of state. Thus ended the guardianship.

And so, those twelve years were wracked with pain, but also with the joy of being there—an experience not always joyful for any parent. The majority of Lee's pain had been inflicted by her family. She could honestly say that she had given herself totally and unselfishly and held out against tremendous odds. These were her decisions and she doubted that many grandmothers would or could do otherwise. Regardless of their constant intervention and criticism, at no time did anyone else come to court to fight for guardianship. The judge once commented that if not for Lee and the trust she secured for them, the girls would most likely have eventually ended up as wards of the court. Lee was sure of one thing—her assertions were documented in the courts. Theirs, formed by malice and jealousy, remained unproven and subject to the laws of karma …

Lee came to the realization that she had made mistakes in listening to some of the advice she had received, such as not defending herself against the slander and not moving away from the negative influences. All that she could do at the time was to make decisions based on all she had to work with then. She learned the players, their character faults, and their agendas. She learned that taking the higher ground could be interpreted as being a doormat. Brittany now had her Master's degree and a job, and Alicia had her Mrs. degree, complete with children. They would do well. She knew that Lana would have approved. She was also smart enough to know that love is its own reward. Love knows no bounds or horizon and is timeless. Her mother's heart would remain open to them. They had always been there and would always be.

CHAPTER 5: The Legacy

White-Glove Ladies

One of the greatest disappointments and revelations related to Lee's work on behalf of domestic violence victims were the white-glove ladies. That's how she referred to women with education and position in the community who took on good causes, but only to the extent that they didn't take their gloves off to get their hands dirty. So many times Lee's attempts to win support to implement changes were met with a personal agenda or political correctness, or a position of defensiveness. Although she would recognize and appreciate all they did to assist women in their reentry into a sane society, she felt blocked by the white-glove ladies. Lee would come to quasi-terms with these feeling years down the road, realizing that their experiences in life might never allow them to feel Lee's passion.

Although all help is welcome, more needs to be done in order to prevent crimes from being committed. If some of these white-glove ladies would use their resources and connections to fight for new and improved legislation, more changes would be seen. Changes will come only when there is as much awareness and education about prevention as there is about criminal defense. Without that, we can expect only perfunctory progress from those in power. Lee knew that. Lana knew that. Sometimes it's a thankless task and an uphill battle, but without these changes we cannot get to the root of the problem.

Lee had joined the local branch of Zonta International, an international women's organization in Marietta within a year of Lana's murder. One of the members of that organization was on the board of the local YLCA. One of Lee's greatest desires was to have a locally held conference on preventive detention programs. She knew where the gaps in the system were and had addressed conferences before. She proposed a conference outline, complete with details dealing with funding, location, and proposed invitees. Her model was a well-implemented domestic violence intervention program. Lee had name-recognition and a background in sales and marketing. She felt that she had the wherewithal to raise funds. With the help of her fellow club members, they sought cosponsorship from the local chapter of this organization. Lee and her team were shocked when the organization refused the proposal. They didn't understand why. Lee had both credibility and a plan. But the organization had its own agenda and wouldn't be taking any direction from her.

Next, Lee courted the local and Influential Senior League of Women for their cosponsorship, sending them the conference outline. After a lengthy interval of time with no reply, Lee finally called them. She was told that "it was a politically sensitive issue, and, by the way, did she know about their domestic violence quilt program?"

At a speaking engagement at a large church, one of the members wanted to help Lee arrange a conference. Not too long into the planning phase, Lee began to learn about the different opinions and agendas of the people involved. The poor person who initially wanted to help Lee was overwhelmed because, as the saying goes, "Everybody wants to get into the act." Yes, everyone has their own agenda; everyone wants to be "politically correct;" everyone who wants to succeed politically "makes nice." And yes, there are issues among women of "thunder stealing" and petty jealousy. Even when she attended a conference in Indianapolis on domestic violence following Lana's nationally reported murder, she heard remarks being made by the prosecutor's office staff about the fact that they worked on the issue all the time, and here Lee was being singled out for recognition.

One of the reasons Lee was so well-respected was because she was able to walk the tightrope over the issue and the realities. She had the ability to verbalize and present herself in a way that attracted politicians because she had the respect and admiration of the community. During one ceremony, U.S. Senator Dan Coats presented her with the pen used by former President George Bush to sign a new bill relating to domestic violence into law. In a personal letter to Lee, Coats noted that Lana's memory and Lee's bravery were the reasons for this new bill.

While she was asked to testify on other state bills, she had determined from the start that no politician would use her for personal reasons, and that she would concentrate on bettering the laws dealing with domestic violence. There were some who wanted to pass "feel good" laws. There were also members of the women's shelter where Lana had worked who really took advantage of the situation and Lana's name, stretching her name past the point of respect in order to bolster their fundraising. Anonymously, people would tell Lee about the shelter's petitioning for huge amounts of money in Lana's name. The shelter went from an older two-story home to a multilevel facility with nice conference rooms. If the end result benefits society, Lee resolved to live with it. Once again, the bottom line is that everyone is tied up with personal agendas, not necessarily with an eye to society's best interests.

That is why Lee wanted to develop a team or a community-coordinated response program. Lee had experienced with Lana the gaps in the system, and she set out to form a commission on domestic violence using a team concept, soliciting the assistance of people from law enforcement, domestic violence shelters, the prosecutor's office, and a State Senator with whom she hoped to work. A pretty prestigious panel. A friend and local attorney, Jean Leyton, was secretary. A local accountant, Ceana Lang, served as treasurer. They incorporated as an organization so that any contributions Lee received from public speaking engagements and other voluntary donations could be placed in the fund to work for domestic violence victims. It was named "The Purple Ribbon Commission Against Domestic Violence." It was not long before she recognized that everyone on the panel wanted to remain blameless for problems in the system. Each member seemed to have his or her own agenda. She felt a sense of disaffection among the members of the panel. Perhaps they felt they had been forced into joining the panel because of public support for Lee?

Lee finally felt that the best contribution she could make was in the arena of public speaking and lobbying. She never solicited a speaking engagement or received any fees. All voluntary contributions went into the fund of the commission. While the panel slowly disintegrated, she kept the commission status active while she continued her public speaking appearances.

Many years later, after moving to Florida, Lee contacted the local Ladies Resource Center and registered as a volunteer. She came to speak to the director and expressed her interest in becoming involved, explaining her background. Lee paved the way for the center to receive the $4,000 lying fallow in the Purple Ribbon Commission's account in Indiana. It was the monies that groups and believers in her mission had donated, and covered the long period of time when she had driven to speaking engagements in a four-state area. Yet Lee never received a letter of acknowledgment of the gift from the Florida chapter. The center told her that she would be able to have some input into decisions on how the funds would be spent. When she called the center later, Lee received an apology, something about computer error, and of course, this was a busy time, and she would receive a call after the holidays. That call never came. It appeared to her that they took the money, blew her off, and threw her away.

On one occasion, she found herself in the ladies room at the blood bank in the same city where she had made this donation. Lee saw a poster and pamphlets with a myriad of contact numbers for women in domestic violence situations and instructions on how to leave safely. Much to her dismay, she realized that they had been placed by another domestic violence group from another city., and not the one she had donated to.

She again contacted the local director and made an appointment. When Lee called to confirm her appointment, she was told that the director had been released from her position two weeks earlier. The center was moving and had opened a large thrift shop.

Lee, undaunted, then contacted the new director and made an appointment to see her. The new director listened to her story and said that she had a position in mind for her and would call. That call never came. A friend and local health professional suggested that Lee contact the local newspaper and gave her the names of two female writers he thought would be interested in the story. She e-mailed them, but never received a response. She had been so accustomed to being respected and wanted. She had simply wanted to help the center. Evidently there is not much domestic violence in this part of Florida, or else it is downplayed, or their work takes a different direction. The treatment she had received at the hands of the Resource Center was one of the biggest disappointments in her life.

While some of her experiences did not lead to the accomplishment of her goals, it cannot be stressed enough that the volunteers of these organizations, at the local, county, and federal levels, represent the victim's lifelines in so many ways. It is of the utmost importance that they are supported and recognized. A huge power lobby could be formed if the separate agencies could, whenever possible, work in tandem to accomplish major goals.

Changes

The publicity of Lana's murder increased the public's awareness of domestic violence. The fact that she was an attractive, intelligent woman who divorced her batterer, put him in jail, and was murdered for it caused a lot of concern. Lana had followed the letter of the law and more. She had put herself through college and divorced her batterer, who had still managed to brutally end her life. She had been chased from her home half-clothed with her children present, and then shot and beaten to death with a terrible viciousness.

The first and closest change was within the local police department. Whereas the police had previously been required to have witnessed the domestic violence, (give me a break, how likely is that?), they were now allowed to document visible signs such as bruises and blood and use that as sufficient evidence to take the offender away.

Numerous local, county, and state policies were initiated in the aftermath of Lana's murder. One of the most important things Lee learned about the legal system is that it can be stated that a certain policy may be in effect, but there is a huge difference between "policy stated" and "policy followed." Unless the "policy" becomes law, it is enforced at the discretion of the agency. When it becomes law, there is more accountability.

Both locally and nationwide, many such changes took place. Lee felt very rewarded by the countless battered women who looked to her to give them a voice. At ceremonies these women would, as one person told Lee, "look at you with love in their eyes, as though you're their angel."

Lee had the capability, experience, and motivation to speak for them. There were also the many people who would express their appreciation for giving them first-hand knowledge of the legal system. One of the most rewarding phrases Lee would hear was, "Because of you," or, "Because of Lana, I have chosen to work on behalf of domestic violence victims." There were also those who left abusive relationships because of Lana's murder.

Now, almost twenty years later, plans for a domestic violence program in the Marietta area in the county where Lana suffered and begged for her life are being explored. They are being spearheaded by a member of the former Purple Ribbon Commission who is now the county commissioner. His plan for a high level conference and domestic violence program almost mirrored Lee's desires. This would be a tribute to Lana and her sisters.

Currently, Federal Bureau of Justice study showed a decline in domestic violence between 1992 and 2004. The study attributes this decline to the 1994 Violence Against Women Act (this act responds to the shortcomings of state justice systems in dealing with violence against women) and better training of law enforcement according to the U. S. Department of Justice Web site.

Recently, a woman in North Carolina who was being stalked and abused, went to the newspaper with her story, and originally they decided not to publish it. Eventually, the paper then did publish the story, which included the name of the victim, the offender, and his past criminal record. The offender responded with twelve bullets to the victim's body as she, like Lana, pounded on a closed door for help.

A victim will sometimes go to the newspaper as a last resort, if everything else fails. She is torn between her fear of reprisal, a real fear of death, and a desperate scream to anyone who can help. Perhaps it is an attempt put the abuser on notice. In the North Carolina case, however, the perpetrator had the decency to kill himself, sparing the family the indignity of the so-called justice system and a squandering of taxpayer dollars.

Indiana has now declared the electric chair to be cruel and inhumane punishment.

Lee knew they would do much better for Adam, and they did—fifteen years after Lana's murder. In his last hours he was allowed to spend time with his family, was given a meal of his choice, and sedative injections. More humane, of course, than Lana's death. Not surprisingly, family members, and often an empathetic public, feel that the perpetrator should experience some of the same suffering as the victim. Instead, they receive fifteen to twenty years of a life lived at the government's expense and a "humane" death. Fair? There is no fair; there's only the system.

Lee hoped that her dream for women like Lana and her countless sisters might come true. Her greatest wish was for true equity in the law, not only for women, but for victims in general—a pretty tall goal. Lana was an innocent bystander, repeatedly subjected to abuse and killed because of the absence of good laws, care, and protection for victims.

Lee had the opportunity to work for victims alongside Indiana Senator Joe Zakas. On the federal level, then Senator, and now Vice

President, Joe Biden has shepherded and held firm the passage of victim's rights acts since 1984, with the successful passage of the Comprehensive Crime Control Act. He is often quoted as saying that he considers the Violence Against Women Act the single most significant legislation that he crafted during his thirty-five-year tenure in the Senate. He was also involved with the improvement of the domestic violence hotline., as stated by one of the Biden Web sites.

From the U. S. Department of Justice Office on Violence Against Women Web site, we read of President Obama's signing an executive order creating the White House Council on Women and Girls. It incorporates the phrase of necessity, "coordinated federal response." It reads:

On March 11, 2009, President Barack Obama signed an Executive Order to establish the White House Council on Women and Girls. Led by the President's Senior Adviser Valerie Jarrett and Director of the White House public Liaison Tina Tchen, the Council will provide a coordinated federal response to the challenges confronted by women and girls and to ensure that all Cabinet and Cabinet-level agencies consider how their policies and programs impact women and families. In its first year, one of the main priorities of the Council will be to work "hand-in-hand with the Vice President, the Justice Department's Office of Violence Against Women, and other government officials to find new ways to prevent violence against women, at home and abroad.

This initial universal attention to women's issues is a ray of hope for all women.

An Open Letter to Women

Lee finished watching a two-hour television program called, "Cops: Crimes Of Passion." It repeatedly showed police responding to domestic violence calls. One woman begged the officer, "No, don't put him in jail. I love him." As the officer put the suspect into the car, she wailed, "I love you, baby. I love you, baby."

The scenario in some areas is that when a domestic violence call is received, regardless of who made it, someone has to be taken into custody. In another scene, the woman was again protesting as the police took the suspect away. She begged the officers, "Don't take him away, it's my fault. I provoked it."

In yet another scene, the woman protested the suspect's being taken away saying, "He pays my bills." And in another, the woman beats on the man who was just trying to leave. Lee wondered who put the program together and why so much of it seemed to be the woman's fault. In all of the scenes, the police were calm and showed no bias. Could it be that the presence of rolling cameras made a difference?

Glaringly absent were the scenes of women like Lana who had left and just wanted to be left alone—the ones who consistently followed the rules and lived in fear of their lives, unable to sleep at night, waiting for the sound of breaking glass, unable to live a respectful and free life. All the women in the documentary involuntarily contributed to Lana's death, because they contributed to the stereotype of the typical battered woman. They set up the system by which there are no red flags for cases like Lana's and so many others. They often used the legal system and the court's time as a weapon of assault or intimidation. This is a stab in the back to women who really live in fear of their lives. This television program accounted for the way outsiders viewed domestic violence and made them respond with the totally innocent question, "Why doesn't she just leave?"

One of the amazing facts is that even women who are married to judges, attorneys, influential or wealthy men who are beating them, will stay because they don't want to lose status or money. Women have so many cards stacked against them and here are their own sisters, confusing the issue. But what kind of a system cannot differentiate between the Saturday night brawlers and the dedicated abuser who makes it his life's mission to control, dominate, harass, stalk, attack, victimize, and destroy? When the victim leaves and stays away and when the abuser continues to follow and abuse, she has a right to protection. The standard order of protection was simply a piece of paper to Adam Portland, and a source of amusement. He knew what he could get away with.

Another option is prevention. The self-imposed identity of a woman who "can't make it on her own" is one that will encourage a woman to pick any man, even if he is the wrong one. It's easy to find the bottom feeders. A recent survey—a collaboration between the men's magazine, *Maxim*, and the women's magazine, *Marie Claire*—asked why women date jerks. The results of the survey were as follows: 13 percent dated guys who are jerks because they thought they could change them; 36 percent said they went out with jerks because being with a schmuck made the sweet moments even sweeter; 77 percent of the women polled said it bothered them when their man checked out other women, but the rest weren't bothered because they knew men "couldn't help it." Need one say more?

No matter how limited her opportunities for male companionship are, being alone is so much better for a woman than being with the wrong man. However, there is no guarantee that even if a woman is attractive, intelligent, and has other options, she won't fall for a handsome and charming con man, especially if she is young and naive. She may also be a person who sympathizes with someone whose background is less than favorable and thinks that his past is in the past, that what she has heard about him is a lie, or that she can reform him. That was Lana's scenario. Don't believe it! The qualities that make a kind and forgiving person will be used against them over and over, and the system will perpetuate that.

When it comes to getting tied up with a man, don't be nice and look for the best in him. Although everyone has some flaws and differences, beware of people who are controlling and intimidating. Attempts to keep you from your friends or family are another red flag. Do not misinterpret these tactics as love. It is not love. It goes without saying that any physical or verbal abuse is a great big red flag. If you have seen this type of behavior within your family, you need to know that it is *not normal*. A relationship should be one of trust, and it should be a safe haven. One of the smartest investments a woman can make is to run a thorough background check on someone she plans to become involved with. If there is any hint or suspicion of his having done something that does not agree with your conscience, morals, or ethics, why not give yourself the time to check that out? Do not fool yourself into thinking you will change him. There is a time in life when the glands are working a lot more than the brain. For a woman, the time window of her highest appeal is much shorter than a man's. A woman shouldn't narrow her window by spending time with a loser. She must give herself the time to become a whole person and time to like herself and the things that she does for herself.

Lana was always self-sufficient and made that one of her most important goals when she advised women at the shelter. For many women, that was all they needed to get away. In Lana's situation, her independence only further enraged Adam Portland. I cannot emphasize enough that each case is individual and should be handled as such, except that we find the cards historically stacked. Remember, Adam Portland said that he only slapped Lana once. There is no such thing as just one slap. Get out! Get out! Get out while the getting is good.

What makes a woman think that, in this vast world filled with millions of men, there isn't anyone better for her? There are national and local help hotlines, and many local organizations that can provide assistance, if needed. If a woman is in a questionable relationship and delays her exit, thinking she can weather the storm, or believing that he will change, it's as though she is getting a sentence of increasingly violent behavior, abuse, and possibly death. It is important that a woman leave smart and safe. There are hotlines that can provide information on how to safely leave an abusive situation. A woman will learn that there are many organizations willing to help. She will learn that love shouldn't hurt. Her first and biggest and bravest and most positively life-shaping and perhaps, life-saving decision she will ever make. The national hotline number is 1-800-799-SAFE.(7233) or 1-800-787-3224 (TTY) 24 hours per day, 7 days a week. If a woman wants to have someone at her side---and she will need someone, she can call Victim's Assitance at 1-800-656-4673. But only she can make that call. A wealth of information and assistance, grant applications for domestic violence programs, contacts, etc., can be found on the U. S. Department Of Justice website, http://www.ovw.usdoj.gov.

Lana's Poems

The following are thoughts, written by Lana. Lee found them in a little spiral notepad while going through her personal possessions after her funeral. She also found some life insurance policies Lana had taken out on herself. The premiums would have been an additional strain on her limited budget, but she had told friends, "If Adam ever gets hold of me, they'll have to bury me in a closed casket." Another promise of Adam's allowed to come to fruition.

My life is like a dead-end street
Having no new roads to try
My road is full of chuckholes
Seems I'm always falling behind.

Maybe someday, though
My life will change
Maybe men will come
And fix my road
To make it free
Of all it's chuckholes.

Make it a highway
Or at least lead to other roads
And then maybe I can come out,
Find a new road
Follow it to where it leads.
And who knows
What I might find—
Maybe a new life, or could it be
To another dead end road?

LOVE IS BETTER

Love, have you ever tried it?
It's better than hate.
It can make you happy. It can give you faith.

Wouldn't it be great

If we could banish hate?
Bring love into the world
Through all the boys and girls.
We could all live together
Loving one another
If we could just
Exterminate hate.

I was here,
Now I am gone.
I left my love to carry on.
If you're sad and alone

And feeling so down
And wish someone was there
To wash off your frown,

Just remember that
There's someone to care.
You may know them and be unaware.

Just remember that everyone is given a chance from above
For everyone is sometimes touched by love.

(Lana Bordolos)

May all be aware of the past and present and work to a better future. May you be touched by Lana's kind of love and become the one who cares for and fixes her road.